# BEFORE I SLEEP . . .

# BEFORE
# I SLEEP...

*The Last Days of*
*Dr. Tom Dooley*

EDITED WITH A FOREWORD BY
## JAMES MONAHAN
*Senior Editor, the* READER'S DIGEST

NEW YORK

*Farrar, Straus and Cudahy*

# CONTENTS

# FOREWORD

On December 14, 1955, a half-dozen *Reader's Digest* editors were hosts at luncheon to a tall, lean, handsome young (28) Navy doctor, Thomas A. Dooley, Lieutenant j.g., who recently had been awarded the Legion of Merit for the singular part he played in the U. S. Navy's heroic peacetime operation "Passage to Freedom" in Indo-China. Tom Dooley began his rapid-fire recital that day even before he sat down at the luncheon table. Two hours later his listeners were still spellbound by the story of his adventures in the wretched refugee camps of Haiphong, where he treated atrocity cases and rescued tortured people from the Communists just as the Red tide engulfed northern Vietnam and the Navy moved a million hapless Tonkinese to safety in the southern city of Saigon.

The *Digest* editors recognized at once that Tom Dooley was a singularly colorful personality with a great story. An agreement was made for its publication. Thus Tom Dooley's notes and diaries (authenticated by Navy Department records) were made into the book *Deliver Us From Evil* which appeared in the spring of 1956.

But even before the book was ready, mercurial Tom Dooley launched a new project. He abandoned his plans to become an orthopedic surgeon and resigned from the Navy. With funds supplied by the *Digest*, plus pharmaceuticals and surgical equipment donated by manufacturers, he organized his own independent medical unit and returned to Indo-China, this time to the Kingdom of Laos, where his services were needed (in the words of Navy corpsman Norman Baker) "by people who ain't got it so good."

Readers of *Deliver Us From Evil* and his second book, *The Edge of Tomorrow* (1958), are familiar with the spiritual transformation of Tom Dooley from a spoiled playboy who might have become a successful society doctor into Dr. Tom Dooley the idealistic, crusading servant of the poor, the sick and the depressed people of Southeast Asia. His third book *The Night They Burned The Mountain* (1960) marked the expansion of his small pilot-plant operation into an organization called Medico which became his lengthening shadow. The same book reached a surprising climax with the disclosure that Tom Dooley at the age of 32 had a serious ailment diagnosed as malignant melanoma, a rare and usually fatal form of cancer. Dr. Dooley was himself now a full-fledged member of what Dr. Albert Schweitzer has called "the fellowship of those who bear the mark of pain."

Between 1955 and 1960 Tom Dooley had become a world famous and somewhat controversial personality. He was admired—and even idolized by some—for his selfless devotion to a high calling, and for his hard-driving way of achieving his goals, often with limited funds and invariably against heavy odds. But he was also criticized, despised and even denigrated by others for his cocky, sometimes overbearing manner and for his tendency to trample on toes and push aside those who got in his way.

Working closely with Tom Dooley during 1955-60, as his *Digest* editor, I saw the many facets of his personality and become familiar with his undeniable faults which, in my opinion, were far outweighed by his many uncommon virtues. He certainly was not a shy person, but neither was he the complete egotist and publicity seeker his critics would make him. The sincerity of his motives and his dedication to his work were obvious to anyone who knew him well.

What impressed me most, and particularly during the last eighteen months of his life, was the relentless drive and the sense of urgency that characterized his activities. That impression became sharper in retrospect after Tom Dooley's death. It seemed that he must have been aware that his days were few, and that he was determined to complete his work or, at least, to put Medico's house in order before his time ran out.

During his last fifteen months, Tom Dooley moved so fast and touched so many places that few people were close to him for any considerable length of time.

Thus, after the shock and sadness of his death had passed, it occurred to some of us that the story of Dooley's last days might be pieced together from the recollections of people who were with him at various times and places. This involved tracking down people from Maine to California, and from Southeast Asia to India and Afghanistan. But when the *Digest* located them they responded wholeheartedly to our appeal for information. The warmth and generosity with which they wrote or told their stories were inspired, obviously, by the depth of their feelings about the man himself.

We are indebted to all of them for the material which makes this book possible. Some are quoted at length, others briefly. More often it has been necessary to incorporate into the general narrative details from what they contributed. Yet the spirit and purpose of each contribution remains.*

This, then, is the story of Tom Dooley's last days, told largely by those who were nearest to him in the events described, beginning with the eyewitnessed cancer operation in August 1959 and ending with the sounding of taps in a snowbound cemetery on January 23, 1961.

James Monahan

* All royalties from the sale of this book have been assigned to Medico, Incorporated, for the continuation and support of the work Dr. Dooley started.

# PART ONE

# 1959:

# SUMMER

# AND FALL

Late on the evening of Monday, August 24, 1959, someone on the ninth floor of Memorial Hospital in New York City scribbled a note which later found its way into the hands of the amused patient: "Doctor Tom Dooley, the famous young jungle medico from Laos, admitted today for major surgery. All is confusion!"

The professional calm of the world's greatest center for cancer research and treatment, which has its own ways of controlling visitors and barring the press, had been disrupted on previous occasions when the presence of famous cancer patients drew reporters, photographers and curiosity-seekers to the hospital lobbies. But since Damon Runyon was there in 1946 and Babe Ruth in 1948, something new had been added to the coverage of such public events—television.

Television moved into Memorial on that August evening in the person of Fred W. Friendly, a tall, thick-lipped, heavy-set man with mournful blue eyes behind thick-lensed glasses, who is the famous producer of documentaries for CBS-TV. For more than three years, Friendly had been brooding over the possibilities of a TV documentary which would present to the American public, truthfully and graphically, the facts about cancer. He wanted to follow one patient's case, with camera and microphone, from diagnosis through surgery to what the doctors call the "prognosis" but which laymen express better with the simple question: "What are the chances?"

The trouble was that the average cancer patient was too sick, too reticent, or too inarticulate for the role; or the doctor or the patient's family and friends balked at publicizing what might well be a personal tragedy. Then, as he browsed through *The New York Times* of Sunday, August 23, Fred Friendly came upon a story signed by Howard A. Rusk, M.D., which seemed to solve his problem: "DR. DOOLEY'S NEW FIGHT: Physician Reluctantly Leaves Jungle Hospital to Become a Cancer Patient."

"I put in a call for Dr. Rusk, who was familiar with our plans for the documentary, and finally reached him about ten o'clock that Sunday night," Fred Friendly recalls. "He was sympathetic but doubtful. He told me that I would first have to obtain the permission of Dr. Dooley, who was then in St. Louis visiting his mother. Then I would have to get the consent of the Memorial board—and Dr. Rusk frankly doubted that they would go for it."

Friendly called Tom Dooley in St. Louis, and Dooley

agreed to cooperate—if CBS-TV could obtain the consent and cooperation of Memorial. At 5:00 P.M. on Monday, August 24, when Tom Dooley entered the hospital, Friendly was waiting for him with a CBS colleague, and a representative of the American Cancer Society. They went directly to a conference room where Memorial's medical board was assembled to consider the unorthodox proposal.

"They probed and questioned and shook their heads," Friendly says. "But the patient was willing, and I think we convinced them that the documentary film we proposed to make would be honest, dignified, scientifically accurate, and would probably become a milestone in public education about cancer. Finally, and very reluctantly, they told us to go ahead. We had to move fast, for Tom Dooley's operation was scheduled for the following morning."

Tom Dooley, the cancer patient, was settled in Room 910 of the hospital, and the ninth floor became chaos even before TV took over. Medico, the organization he had founded with Dr. Peter Comanduras in 1957 was in the process of getting a friendly divorce from the International Rescue Committee, the original sponsoring organization, and would henceforth operate as an independent unit. So, from the moment Dooley arrived, he had a steady stream of visitors— lawyers, Medico doctors, secretaries, and aides lugging letter files, typewriters, dictating machines. To the doctors and nurses, Thomas A. Dooley, suffering

5

from a generally fatal form of cancer, was a decidedly unique case in medical history.

Sometime after 7:00 P.M., Tom Dooley's doctors took over, and the Medico people were shooed off to get some dinner. When they returned, shortly before 9:00 P.M., the ninth floor corridor was strewn with cables and blocked by electronic equipment and TV technicians. Inside Room 910 the bright lights glared, the microphones were open, and the camera was rolling. CBS reporter Howard K. Smith was well along in the opening interview of the unrehearsed documentary, "Biography of a Cancer."

"Let me ask you something," Smith was saying, "which you need not answer if you don't want to. Does it cause you physical pain?"

Seated in the hospital bed, skinny, hollow-cheeked Tom Dooley, wearing TV make-up and looking young and rakish in blue pajamas, raised his eyebrows and gave Smith a wry smile.

"It causes me *discomfiture*," he said.

"What is the likely future in a case like yours?"

"You go downstairs and ask *them*. They'll tell you."

"Doctor Dooley, you seem to be taking this in a very—almost a blithe way. Do you really feel that way?"

"I'd be kind of stupid if I got *too* concerned about it, wouldn't I? You know, I'm scared to death of this thing becoming *maudlin*. I'm scarced to death that you'll depict my cancer as a clutching, agonizing sort

6

of thing. . . . Sure, anybody who's got cancer has got some discomfort. But I don't want anybody to get sloppy over this. I don't want any of that 'dying doctor's agony' stuff. That's—that's stupid!"

"Well, Doctor, you have let us come in and interview you on the eve of a serious operation. Tell me, why did you let us do that?"

"That I can explain easily. When I was an interne, I saw a lot of things. There's a tremendous amount of ignorance here—just like we have ignorance in my village in Laos where the people believe in witchcraft and sorcery. There's ignorance in America about the word 'cancer.' The minute they hear the word 'cancer' Americans think of gloom, doom and death. This makes patients mentally crippled even before they get to the hospital. It puts them in a bad state of mind before surgery. It handicaps the doctor's ability to deal with them. . . . Maybe, in a small way, I can make the people who see this show, and who know that Dooley's got cancer—maybe in a small way I can make them see that they need not have as much fear of the word 'cancer' as they have had in the past. . . ."

The camera and microphone caught it all. Here was one man who needed no coaching, no Tele-Prompter, no "idiot cards." Tom Dooley was, as one technician remarked, "a natural."

"The second reason why I'm doing this is pure selfishness. I want this chance to talk to some twenty- or twenty-five million Americans about the work of

7

Medico. I want to tell them how we are trying to send doctors and nurses and corpsmen to the farthest outposts of the world to take care of sick people who 'ain't got it so good.' For the next few weeks I'm going to let you photograph me inside and outside because maybe that will give me a chance also to tell Americans how we at Medico need their help. . . . For these reasons, you're welcome in Room 910 tonight."

*August 25.* Next morning, the draped, anesthetized figure of Tom Dooley lay motionless on the operating table in the middle of Memorial's big surgical amphitheatre, and the capped, robed, masked figures of the surgical team began the long, meticulous ritual of surgery. From an observer's enclosure, the CBS cameras, equipped with special lenses, caught every detail, even peering over the surgeon's shoulder.

Standing beside Howard K. Smith in the glass-enclosed gallery overlooking the operating room, Dr. Henry T. Randall, Medical Director of the Memorial Cancer Center, explained that what was going on was really a preliminary operation.

"The idea of what they're doing here is to find out how far the cancer has spread. You recall Dr. Dooley said that he'd had a lump on his chest just below his shoulder. That lump was taken from there, and from that tissue the original diagnosis was made. Now he has some swelling of the lower part of his chest and in some of the cord-like structure under the skin. We can't be certain whether those lumps are cancer or whether they actually represent an injury or secondary effect of an injury. So the purpose of this operation, well away from where the lump was taken out, is to find out whether or not the cancer may have spread to this area. If it has spread way down to where they're taking out tissue now, then the disease will have gone beyond the point where it will be possible to remove it surgically. Whereas if there's no cancer in this area, then they will do a major operation within the next couple of days."

"So, they're trying to isolate the cancerous area?"

"Exactly, to find out how far it's gone, and, hopefully, how far it hasn't gone."

"I understand the form of cancer that Dr. Dooley has is called melanoma. What exactly is melanoma?"

"Melanoma is a very malignant and, fortunately, a very rare kind of cancer. . . . The biopsy specimen is almost out now and they're about to send it down to our pathology laboratory. I think you'd like to go down and see how they handle the diagnosis of whether or not there's cancer in it."

Later, from the pathology laboratory, Howard K. Smith explained: "With the conclusion of the exploratory operation, it now seemed that the malignancy, originating near the shoulder, had not spread down to the suspicious area from which the piece of tissue had been removed. The problem of treating Dr.

9

Dooley's cancer was still an urgent one, but there was hope now for dealing with it surgically, by means of a second and more extensive operation."

*August 26.* Between operations, Howard K. Smith went back to Room 910 and asked Dooley how he felt about the prospects.

"Well, it's a perfectly natural reaction to have a certain amount of apprehension before you get carved on—doubly so if you're a doctor. But on the other hand I've got a great deal of faith and confidence in the people who are taking care of me."

"Well, what about the future? Do you plan to go back to Laos?"

"I plan to go back to Laos. I want to get another clinic going. I hope to get a small airplane from somebody and use this to set up a clinic at a village called Ban Houei Sai. I've got so much to do right now that I'm not particularly thinking about any length of time. Some people may say, 'Well, Dooley, you've got a year to go—you'd better hurry.' Or they may say, 'Dooley, you've got five years to go.' I don't know. I'm just going to live like I was told long ago—live as though you're going to die tomorrow. I'm not bleak about it, nor do I feel particularly blithe about it. I realize my case is serious, but I also realize that the doctors are doing a pretty tremendous job, and with the luck of the Irish, and by the Grace of God, I'll make it O.K."

*August 27.* The cameras once again were focused on the surgically draped figure lying in the middle of the huge amphitheatre, and Howard K. Smith and Dr. Randall were back at their posts in the glass-enclosed gallery.

"We are now concerned with removing the skin and tissue in the area where this lump first appeared," Dr. Randall explained, "because it was just shelled out by his friend in Laos. In order to remove the first logical root of spread, we have to remove the glands, back up under the armpit, and sufficient skin and tissue including muscle . . . so that a complete layer all the way around the original point has been taken out surgically."

As the operation progressed, the undraped portion of Dooley's torso began to resemble a bushel basket overflowing with hardware.

"Doctor," Smith asked, "what is that forest of instruments there for?"

"Well, those are clamps. We call them clamps or hemostats, if you will. They're like little pairs of pliers, except they have a lock on the handle. You put them on the end of a blood vessel, after you have cut through it, clamp it down, and it stays there, hanging onto the end of the blood vessel, until you have time to tie a thread around it. Then the clamp is taken off, leaving the little silk ligature or suture in its place."

"How long do you expect this operation's going to take, approximately?"

11

"An operation of this sort, involving the placing of skin graft on the chest wall to fill in the wide area of skin that's being removed, will take on the order of three hours and a half or so. . . ."

Nearly four hours later the masked surgeon looked up from the vast, gaping but virtually bloodless surgical wound on Dooley's chest. The microphone picked up his voice: "I've felt a great deal of pity for this young guy. He has a malignant disease. He knows it. And he's been trying to act as though it didn't bother him in the slightest. This, for a physician, is a most trying and almost impossible feat. Today, for the first time, he admitted that he was beginning to be worried a little bit, and I told him I was very happy that he was appearing so normal. . . . All right, here's the surgical specimen out fine. We got all the bleeders."

When the operation was over, Howard K. Smith asked Dr. Randall: "From what you know of the case what would you say about his chances?"

"His immediate surgical chances are excellent. Unless something totally unforeseen happens, he's going to be all right within a few days. He'll be out of the hospital in about ten days, I would guess. We'll know in about a week what the glands under the arm show. That's pretty important. . . . If there is no spread we can detect, this would be the best outlook for him. But we have to remember that melanoma spreads in two ways. It spreads to the lymph nodes, but it spreads into the blood too. It's impossible to tell now—and

only careful follow-up will give us the answer—
whether his melanoma has spread through the blood,
and may be growing in tiny spots in his lungs or liver
or other vital organs."

*August 30.* Tom Dooley was sitting up in bed, answering the great accumulation of mail, receiving visitors,
and participating in the endless conferences concerning the future of Medico.

He impatiently riffled through the piles of mail,
and pulled out a few airmail letters with recognizable
foreign stamps. The first one he opened was from
Dwight Davis, one of Dr. Dooley's staff in Laos, written in Muong Sing about a week before. Dwight
apologized for having lied in order to induce Dooley
to obey Dr. Peter Comanduras' mysterious order of
August 15 to return to the United States immediately,
when Dwight knew the facts about the cancer diagnosis, which were being concealed from Dooley at
the time.

"Forgive us for having to practice a deception on
you," Dwight Davis wrote. "I am sure you know that
it had to be done that way or we would not have
done it.

"What I want to say now is this: We are more proud
than you will ever realize at being members of the
first Medico team out in the field. We intend to fill
your shoes to the best of our ability until you come

13

back here, as you certainly will. Earl and I want you to concentrate on getting well, and not upon worrying about your hospital. . . ."

There was another long typewritten letter from Muong Sing, written by Dwight on behalf of all the members of the hospital team. The purpose was to give Dr. Dooley a complete report on what had transpired since his departure, and to assure him that everything in the hospital was under control.

"We are sure that you remember the man who used to come here with his son, the little 12-year-old blind boy. Well, the man came back not long ago, bringing his blind son with him. The father said that, since he lives so far away, he wanted to stay here with us for a while and try to kick the opium habit!

"We hired him to work around the place. . . . Of course, we doubt if he is worth it, but he does try to do some work, and he really is slowing down on the *ya fin* (opium)!

"Earl [Rhine] let the blind boy hold our little gibbon (who is also blind), and they took to each other as though they were old friends. It was a tragic and yet beautiful thing to see the two of them playing together. I am sure that the little blind gibbon knows, somehow, that the boy is also blind, because it never tries to bite him, whereas, as you know, that gibbon takes a nip out of everyone who comes near him.

"Both of your eye cases are doing well. Our friend with the leech inside his nose still has it there. The

Meo man and woman are doing well and will be going home soon. The little boy with the bad lip is better. . . ."

The entire staff—Chai, Sai, Vong, Ooh La, and the others placed their signatures, in Lao script, beside their typewritten names. All, that is, except Fang-Son-of-Claw, and Sam-The-Killer-Bear, who merely placed an "X" beside their names.

Tom was in high spirits, brimming with confidence, and eager to get out of the hospital. His announced plans dismayed his doctors: Ten days or two weeks in Hawaii, then eight weeks of barnstorming up and down the United States, raising funds for Medico. He was determined to be back in Muong Sing for Christmas.

The CBS cameras and microphones were still very much in evidence, but there were some amusing incidents which the cameras failed to catch. For instance, one day a Dooley admirer in Memorial, an elderly English gentleman, telephoned for information and was informed that Dooley was feeling fine. The admirer was invited to come right up. As he came down the ninth-floor corridor, leaning heavily on a cane, he was horrified to see Tom Dooley being wheeled out toward the operating room on a stretcher. Dooley recognized the visitor and laughed: "Don't let them scare you, Daddy-O! This is just a retake for the television film we're making."

*September 4.* The CBS cameras rolled for the last time in Memorial Hospital as Tom Dooley had a final talk with his surgeon.

"Well, Tom, I've got some good news for you. The report from the Pathology Department indicates that there is absolutely no evidence of this disease anywhere in the tissues that I removed in operation."

"Everything negative? Nodes? Muscles? Thigh? Everything?"

"You sound like a Doubting Thomas. I wouldn't ordinarily show a pathology report to a patient, because it wouldn't mean anything to him. But I'll show it to you so that you know that I'm not holding back from you. . . . I know, when you're a doctor, you have certain ideas about yourself—that you're different from other people. We think we're immortal sometimes, but—"

"I didn't feel that way last week."

"You see, Tom, being a doctor, and knowing the diagnosis in advance, you were sure that everything that was not right in any part of your body was part of this disease. Therefore, we took many examinations to prove whether you had any evidence of spread or not. Now, for instance, you were so concerned about your arm. . . . That proved to be entirely the result of that injury you had before."

"But then, I had the cancer—the primary cancer. . . . And we got that early, because we felt the lump. Within a couple of months after the first development, we had it taken out. . . . And then when I came here you found no extension anywhere else?"

"No extension anywhere else."

"Well, would it be like saying that I had pneumonia, and I took penicillin, and I got cured of the pneumonia, and my pneumonia is finished? Do I—will I get 'pneumonia' again?"

"Because you've known so much about your own case—much more than the average lay patient would —it has been possible to speak utterly and completely frankly about things which, under ordinary circumstances, might be frightening—almost terrifying—to an ordinary patient. And yet here you and I are talking about them as if they were occurring to somebody else and not to you. Now, to say that this was just like another attack of pneumonia would be ridiculous. It wouldn't be fair to you or to me, but especially not to yourself. On the other hand, we can say that this condition was eradicated in a very wide, radical manner, almost as soon as it could possibly have been done, after the diagnosis was established. . . ."

"Which is on my side?"

"Which is all on your side. And I would say this— there's no reason why you shouldn't anticipate a better than even break."

"Then you are saying that if a primary cancer like this is cut out, as full and well as this has been cut out, and if everything comes out negative; then there's no sense in my even thinking about living one year or two years or five years or ten years—just go ahead and continue living each day as I should?"

"Just as you always have, Tom—I think that's always been your policy, hasn't it?"

Dooley nodded, thoughtfully. "Walt Whitman, I think, said that it's not so important what you do with the *years* of your life, but it's very important how you use each *hour*. That's how I'll live."

*Editor's note:* When "Biography of a Cancer" was broadcast over the CBS television network on Thursday evening, April 21, 1960, Dr. Tom Dooley was back in Southeast Asia. Later, Fred W. Friendly's documentary won the Albert and Mary Lasker Medical Journalism Award for the outstanding medical television feature of 1960.

*September 7.* Tom Dooley decided to leave Memorial Hospital on Labor Day. Whether this was an impulsive decision on his part, or whether he had kept his plans secret in order to avoid fuss and arguments, no one seems to know. But Teresa Gallagher, one of the most devoted of Tom Dooley's volunteer aides, was shocked when she found that no preparations for the move had been made.

"So I just brought my old 1950 Hudson into the city," Teresa recalls. The city seemed deserted on that warm holiday morning. "In the hospital, all the hubbub of the past few weeks had died down. There was one *Life* photographer still there taking pictures, but otherwise no one was around. We cleared out Room 910, and stacked Tom's baggage and books on a couple of hand trucks. We also had three shopping bags full of mail—later I found that one of them was full of money! We came out of Memorial lugging two bronze busts, both by Leo Cherne. One of Dr. Albert Schweitzer, and the other of Lincoln. The Lincoln bust had been sent by mistake when Tom asked Mr. Cherne for a bust of Schweitzer. We piled all this stuff into my car, and drove to the Waldorf.

"Tom had his arm in a black silk sling. He was very thin, but he looked so much better than when he first went into the hospital. He seemed full of drive, alertness, determination, hope. There was no sign of illness. He never winced or indicated pain in any way. We knew he felt a lot of post-operative pain and soreness. Once, he showed us the huge skin graft on his chest— it looked exactly like a raw sunburn. We wondered how he could move about with it and not even wince or say 'ouch.'"

Teresa helped Tom get settled at the Waldorf in a corner room that looked enormous upon his arrival, but which soon seemed inadequate as it became cluttered with his paraphernalia and the incoming mail sacks. Then Teresa left to drive back to Jamaica in the old Hudson.

"Shortly after Dr. Dooley left Memorial and came to the Waldorf," says Ann Walsh, Publicity Director of the Waldorf, "was when I met Teresa Gallagher for the first time. But I soon got to know her better and to admire her as one of the most remarkable girls I have ever known. Teresa is a deeply religious person; but, more than that, she is one of those rare, dedicated people who can never be happy unless they are quietly and unostentatiously engaged in some good works.

"From Dr. Dooley's books, and from what he told me later that morning, I knew Teresa was a secretary in the New York headquarters of the Metropolitan Life Insurance Company. She first became acquainted with his work when she read *Deliver Us From Evil,* his first book. Later, when he went to Laos, she organized a Dooley Aid Club with her fellow workers in the Metropolitan Life office. The club held little parties and benefits and collected several thousand dollars which they sent to Tom Dooley to support his work.

"I believe Teresa and Dr. Dooley met face-to-face for the first time when he was in New York in 1958. Thereafter she was his most devoted follower, and she used practically all her spare time working as a Medico volunteer—raising funds, running errands, and taking care of Dr. Tom Dooley's growing volume of mail.

"One morning that I called on Dr. Tom and found him trying to sort out and open the stacks of mail. 'How can I ever cope with this?' he asked, looking at me helplessly. Then he snapped his fingers, and said,

20

'There's only one way to handle this! I simply must have Teresa.'

"He couldn't find his little address book, and finally asked me to look up the Metropolitan Life telephone number in the book. He tried to reach Mr. Ecker, the president, and then talked to a vice president he seemed to know fairly well.

"I had heard about Tom Dooley's way of boldly asking for what he wanted, and invariably getting what he asked for. But this was the first time I had ever seen him in operation, and I was frankly amused. As I recall, he said, 'Look, I am desperately in need of help, and I believe you are the only one who can help me. I want you to get the Metropolitan to give Teresa Gallagher a leave of absence so that she can work for me for a while. I know she's got about twelve years seniority there, and I don't want her to lose that. I also know how much she earns. I'll be willing to pay her the same salary unless' (and here Tom gave me a wink) 'unless the Metropolitan would care to give her a leave of absence with pay—I repeat *with pay*. See what you can do, please. You'll really be doing me the greatest possible service.'

"Then he hung up the phone and heaved a great sigh of relief, as if certain that the matter was settled, in his favor."

Teresa Gallagher was at her typewriter one morning when she looked up and saw Dr. Tom Dooley being ushered into the office of Mr. James E. McGurk, for

21

whom she worked. A few moments later she was called in.

"There was Dr. Dooley on his knees pleading to Mr. McGurk—'Please Mr. McGurk, can I borrow your secretary for six months?' He was always such a prankster.

"They argued back and forth, good-naturedly, with Tom insisting on six months, and Mr. McGurk saying that he couldn't spare me for more than thirty days. They finally settled on a three months leave of absence. Tom told me later that he believed in always asking for the impossible and settling for less. Three months, he said, would be plenty of time in which to clean up the mail, get the new Medico office started, and finish up his fund-raising tour.

*September 8.* Dooley had been told confidentially (by Dr. Charles W. Mayo, Chairman of the Board of Judges) that he had been chosen to receive the 1959 Criss Award by Mutual of Omaha. This was a high professional honor, bestowed in previous years upon such outstanding American doctors as Jonas Salk and Howard A. Rusk. Now he learned that the 1959 Criss Award would be given unusual prominence because it coincided with the 50th anniversary of Mutual of Omaha. The presentation was to be made at a banquet in Omaha, before a star-studded dais, and broadcast over a nationwide television hookup.

At 4:00 P.M. on September 8, he met a group of

Mutual of Omaha executives at the Waldorf. They had come to discuss arrangements for the Award Dinner, and also to look him over. When he was invited to remain for supper, Tom Dooley's reaction was characteristic. "No, I have to run along in just a few minutes," he said. "Let's get this over with."

Time passed, and Dooley, now immersed in the Criss Award project, made no move to leave.

"Along about eight o'clock," Bob Copenhaver of Mutual's press department recalls, "we reminded him that, while we did not want to see him go, he did have another appointment. Tom just laughed. 'That appointment was just an excuse to get away in case I didn't like you,' he said. 'But now I like you fine. And I have been worrying for the past hour or so if you would invite me again to dinner.'"

The party adjourned to a nearby restaurant and ordered dinner. During dinner Tom Dooley disclosed his plans for the months ahead. He would go to Hawaii for two weeks' rest, returning to New York on October 9. Then he would start out on a sixty-day lecture tour to raise money for Medico.

Bob Copenhaver was assigned to "cover" the first two dates in Hartford, Connecticut, and Holyoke, Massachusetts, and get to know Tom better. Says Copenhaver: "And that's how I became a 'Cooley for Dooley.'"

He arrived in Honolulu, and went directly to the Reef Hotel. For the next two weeks he spent most of his time fussing and worrying over the revision of his book, *The Night They Burned the Mountain*. Few people recall seeing him during this interlude. William Lederer and Gene Burdick, co-authors of *The Ugly American*, came to see him, and found him in good spirits and looking fine. He gave a few talks, raised some money for Medico. Probably the one who saw most of him was Mrs. Norma Spring, a devoted Dooley volunteer who served as a sort of "Teresa Gallagher of the Islands."

Mrs. Spring is a woman in her 60's, with two sons about Tom's age, and he was devoted to her. He loved to tease her, and sometimes to shock her by telling outlandish tales. Dooley had already concocted the line he was to use whenever anyone asked about his operation: "Where the nipple used to be, I'm now growing a knee."

Says Bill Lederer: "People had to figure out for themselves this referred to the fact that a large area of tissue had been dermatomed from his leg, just above the knee, and grafted onto his chest where the radical mastectomy [breast removal] had been performed. Anyhow, Tom considered this a good joke, although I'm pretty sure that most of the time the facts involved were really no laughing matter. Tom told me that it was always a toss-up as to which hurt most— his chest or his leg. He had abandoned the black silk sling, but now he habitually supported his sore right arm against his chest with his left hand. He was also walking with a noticeable limp."

Thus, the Hawaiian interlude probably wasn't much of a vacation. But it was the nearest thing to relaxation he would know from that day forward.

*October 9.* He spent the day in New York, looked in at the new Medico office, said "This is exactly what Bedlam must have been," and retired to his room at the Waldorf.

"This was Room 330 in the Graybar Building," says Teresa Gallagher, "which William Zeckendorf had donated rent free until April 1960, after which Medico would pay regular rent. The Metropolitan Life had given us some discarded desks and chairs and we bought other things secondhand.

"Working there was a rugged experience. There were some salaried employees and many volunteers. The mail kept pouring in—once we received five mail sacks in one day—and everybody was sitting in somebody else's lap, and people would have to leave the room when we wanted to open the file drawers.

"I had been working there full time since mid-September, but I found it easier to get Dr. Tom's mail done at night when only the volunteers were working in the office.

"Fortunately, at about this time, Mr. Paul Hellmuth, the young Boston lawyer, who is also a trustee of Notre

Dame, became interested in Medico. One day he came in and sat in the waiting room, surrounded by mail sacks, crates of pharmaceuticals, filing cases, and cardboard boxes containing dolls and toys and clothing for the kids in Laos. Mr. Hellmuth agreed with Dr. Comanduras that Medico would have to acquire more floor space and reorganize the office force. He helped us find a larger suite of offices on the fourth floor of the Graybar Building.

"Meanwhile, I had talked over the problem of Doctor Tom's personal mail (which was my job) with Tommy Earl, one of the men in my department at the Metropolitan. Tommy and his friends got me a Sound-Scriber—a dictating machine that isn't much bigger than a shoe-box.

"On that same day that Doctor Tom had taken one look at the office and fled, I took the SoundScriber up to the Waldorf. 'Look,' I said, 'this is the answer. It runs on batteries and you can take it with you wherever you go, and mail the discs back to me. Try it.'

"Of course, you know what happened. That little gadget was the greatest joy to him during his last days. I can't even guess how many hundreds of discs he sent us or how many thousands of letters we transcribed from them. He never could have operated without it. And no matter where he was, the girls on the 'Dooley Disc Team' would hear his voice right up to the end when he was too sick to talk."

26

*October 10.* Dooley started his barnstorming tour in Hartford; two days later when he finished the engagement in Holyoke, Massachusetts, he decided that Bob Copenhaver was indispensable. He telephoned Mr. V. J. Skutt, president of Mutual of Omaha: "V. J., I'll let you keep the ten thousand bucks that go with the Criss Award if you will lend me Bob Copenhaver as press secretary for the rest of this tour." Of course, Dooley got Copenhaver—and the prize money too.

Bob Copenhaver had gone to Holyoke merely as an observer. But, as an experienced newspaper man and an expert in public relations, he could not resist the temptation to take over when he saw Dooley, a sick man despite his apparent exuberance, trying to cope with reporters, photographers, reception committees, and the inevitable horde of well-wishers and autograph seekers. He took charge of the press conference in Holyoke, and Dooley, who considered himself an old hand at dealing with the press, was amazed to see how smoothly things went.

For the next seven or eight weeks Bob Copenhaver was a "Cooley for Dooley." He arranged transportation, handled baggage, paid bills, dealt with the press, and spent what time was left arranging and criticizing Dooley's speeches, and trying to convince Tom that much of his unfavorable publicity stemmed directly from his flippant way of talking to people and particularly to the press.

The lecture tour was made up of mostly one-night

stands. They were seldom in any spot for more than two days. For Bob Copenhaver the experience was both an eye opener and exhausting.

"Tom always took off at the crack of dawn, and he never touched down again until the wee hours of the next morning. He never paused, never rested between breakfast, luncheon and dinner engagements. There were always more people who had to be seen, or something else that had to be done. After a late evening engagement, if we weren't catching a plane, he would want to work on his manuscript, or he would get out that damn dictating machine. Half the time I would be so groggy that I'd try to make a break for my own room. Tom would say, 'No, stick around, I want you to hear this.'

"Even then Tom seemed to have a sort of pathological resentment that there were only twenty-four hours in a day. Once, I remember, we quit working along about two o'clock in the morning and we had to catch a plane at seven. I was half dead, but Dooley, the sick man, was fresh as a daisy. 'Isn't it a shame, Bob,' he asked, 'that human beings have to waste so much precious time on sleep?' "

Once, while they were on the West Coast, Copenhaver recalls, they returned to the hotel after a dinner and late reception for Dooley and found a telegram from the editors demanding clarification and additional material for a chapter of the book. Dooley ordered Bob to get a stenographer in a hurry.

Says Bob: "I called all the public stenographers and services in the phone book, but of course none answered. Finally I called the guy who had been in charge of the dinner that evening. He called back and said that he had phoned his own secretary and that she was now on her way to the hotel.

"I met her in the lobby. Wow! She was a knockout—about twenty-four, pretty as a picture, wearing some kind of a silk scarf around her head. I took her up to Tom's suite and opened the door.

"Tom took one look and panicked. 'Get her out of here before someone sees her,' he whispered. 'Who in hell would believe she's up here *taking dictation* at this hour of the morning?'

"So—we went downstairs, and the three of us worked in a corner of the lobby until five A.M.!"

*November 2.* On Monday morning Dooley addressed the students of Phillips Exeter Academy in New Hampshire. At noontime he was at the Sacred Heart Academy in Newton, Massachusetts. In the afternoon he spoke at Boston College before driving to Worcester to address the assembled undergraduates of Holy Cross College. There a big surprise was in store for him.

The Very Reverend Wilham A. Donaghy, S.J., President of Holy Cross, bestowed upon Tom Dooley

the honorary degree of doctor of science. In conferring
the degree Father Donaghy said:

Modern man has lost the old concept of pain as a
sacramental mystery, a participation in the Passion, a
means whereby the member can become more like the
thorn-crowned Head. In the Christian scheme of things
pain was not merely to be anesthetized but canonized.
It was not only a cause of misery but a chance for merit.
Saints prayed for it and received it with resignation and
even rejoicing in the dear ingenuous old days before
aspirin so largely supplanted aspiration. . . .

All of us know the Hippocratic Oath; but I suspect
that even in this learned gathering there might be a
few who are unaware that Hippocrates also wrote "The
Precepts." Mind you, now, this is roughly 2300 years
ago! "Sometimes," intoned this sage old man, "give your
services for nothing, calling to mind a previous benefac-
tion or present satisfaction. For where there is love of
man, there is also love of the art. For some patients,
though conscious that their condition is perilous, re-
cover their health simply through their contentment
with the goodness of the physician. . . ." Doctor Thomas
Anthony Dooley could reach across the centuries and
call Hippocrates "Brother."

*November 9-11.* Omaha, Nebraska, seemed to Tom
Dooley like a carnival town when they checked into
the Frontenelle Hotel at 5:00 A.M. on Monday morning, November 9. Everywhere he saw signs of prepara-
tion for the Mutual of Omaha Criss Award celebration
with Tom Dooley, of course, as the central figure.

30

"It was quite a job for me to convince him that he ought to get a few hours sleep before we plunged into the heavy schedule of events leading up to the award dinner the following evening," says Copenhaver. "We had a two-bedroom suite with a parlor in between. I went into my room and closed the door. Less than four hours later Tom was there, fully dressed, shaking me and reminding me that we had a press conference right after breakfast."

From the press conference, held in the home office of Mutual of Omaha, they went to a reception and luncheon in Dooley's honor at Creighton University, and after the luncheon they toured Boys' Town. There was a late afternoon reception for 1200 business and civic leaders held in Mutual of Omaha's large auditorium, and that evening Mutual's president, V. J. Skutt, gave a small informal dinner in his home for Dr. Dooley, Mrs. Agnes Dooley, Dr. and Mrs. Charles W. Mayo, Mrs. Earl Rhine, Mrs. Dwight Davis, the Copenhavers and several Mutual directors.

Tuesday, November 10, was Dooley's big day. After a family breakfast he addressed 200 wives of Mutual executives and general agents, and then went to the Omaha Civic Auditorium where the dinner and presentation were to be held that night, and participated in the rehearsal of the televised portion of the proceedings. Two giant screens had been erected behind the long dais so that the 2000 guests could witness the nation-wide telecast in which they were also participants.

Arthur Fiedler, director of the famous Boston Pops Orchestra, had flown in to conduct the Omaha Symphony Orchestra that evening. At the rehearsal, Tom Dooley spotted the distinguished, silver-maned conductor and ran the full length of the huge auditorium and threw his arms around him. Later he took Fiedler to luncheon—hamburgers at a nearby Snack Shack.

In the afternoon he was supposed to address Mutual employees and general agents in the company auditorium. Copenhaver, now nervously acting as guardian and major domo, had trouble keeping Tom in tow. "The pixie in Dooley was riding high that afternoon. When the time came for his speech, I couldn't find him anywhere. I made a hasty search of the building and found him in the mailing department surrounded by ecstatic females and fouling up the stamp machines. 'Go away, Copenhaver,' he said. 'If I stay around here for a while longer they're going to let me play real Post Office.'"

At 5:45 that afternoon Dooley started to dress for dinner. He had lost his suspenders, so he stole Bob Copenhaver's and told Copenhaver to go scare up another pair. Then they went to a reception at the Omaha Athletic Club for the distinguished guests: Dr. Charles W. Mayo, General Jimmy Doolittle, DeWitt Wallace, Fred Astaire, Dr. Louis M. Orr, President of the A.M.A., Prince Souphan, son of the

King of Laos, and the Hon. Khamchan Pradith, Chargé d'affaires of the Royal Lao Embassy in Washington.

The dinner that night was climaxed by the presentation of the Criss Award to Dr. Thomas A. Dooley

Dooley's remarks were brief and modest; for once the glowing tributes from Dr. Mayo, General Doolittle, President Skutt and others seemed to have taken the gusty Dooley breath away. But after the presentation had been made he could not resist the opportunity to wave the $10,000 check at the television cameras and assure everyone that it was real. The money, he said, would go toward the establishment of a Medico hospital in Africa. He took much of the one-and-a-half minutes allotted to him to introduce Emily Rhine and Esperanza Davis and to praise their husbands, Earl and Dwight, who were still running his hospital in the mountains of northern Laos.

Following the dinner and telecast, there was a small reception for the Criss Award judges and the officers of Mutual of Omaha. It had been a tremendous day, yet Tom Dooley showed no signs of fatigue.

"Omaha is my home town," says Bob Copenhaver. "But do you suppose I could go home and get some sleep? Not a chance! We sat up until five o'clock the next morning, revising the complicated war chapter of his book, and then caught a nine o'clock flight for Lincoln, Nebraska, and some more speeches."

33

*December 2.* They reached St. Louis, Missouri, Dooley's home town and the last scheduled stop on the tour. The Junior Chamber of Commerce (the Jaycees) had arranged a dinner for Dooley which was attended by nearly 1000 people. On the dais were many distinguished doctors, clergyman, civic leaders, and Prince Souphan, Khamchan Pradith, and Dr. Thongphet, of Vientiane.

Dooley was in top form that night. He assured his audience that "vast economic-aid programs that provide high dams and express highways will never satisfy the hunger and thirst and the desperate need of the people of Asia." The answer to such needs, he said, would have to come from individual Americans reaching out to the people of Asia. "Which brings us to Medico, the organization Dr. Comanduras and I started in 1957."

However, Dooley said, "too many noble words have been said about Medico. Too many people have honored us with the noble statements. But there are too many people who blather and bleat about such things. That's the trouble—the meaning has been drained out of the noble pronouncements we Americans make about the world we live in. The meaning has been drained out of words like 'freedom' and 'democracy' and 'love.' The time has come when you and I, and especially the kids in our schools and colleges, must put back into those words their original meaning. The time has come, as President Eisenhower

34

has so magnificently stated, for us to start using not just the *words* of peace, but also the *works* of peace.

"We, in Medico, know that we can perform the works of peace, because that is what Medico has been doing since it was founded in 1957. We, in Medico, simply go out and take care of sick people in parts of the world where medical care is almost entirely unknown. We take care of them simply and unselfishly. By our deeds, and not by words, we demonstrate what is really in the hearts of the American people. We don't stand up on a platform and talk to them through microphones and loudspeakers. We go into an Asian village and live with the people. We treat their ills, we help to deliver their babies, we go to their weddings, we attend their funerals. We speak to them in a language that they can understand. We don't have to tell them we love them. They know we love them, because if we didn't love them we wouldn't be there ministering to their pathetic needs. Thus, they grow to love us, not just as individuals, but as living symbols of America—the only America they really know. That is why I believe that we in Medico are restoring genuine meaning to words like 'freedom' and 'democracy' and 'love' for the people of Southeast Asia. We are doing this for you, and if you really believe in what we are doing, you can make your conviction felt through Medico."

Dooley looked around at the prominent clergymen seated on the dais, and assured them that he was *not*

35

in the business of religious proselytizing. "Out of the thousands of letters Medico gets every day, there are always a dozen or more that come addressed to the Rev. Dr. Thomas A. Dooley, S.J.! Just because my name happens to be Dooley! I want to make it perfectly plain that we are *not* in the business of converting anybody to anything. We are not out to make mackerel-snapping Irish Catholics out of happy, contented Buddhists." (Here he turned to a prominent Catholic priest seated on the dais.) "We are in the business of treating sick people, dear Father. Converting people to Catholicism is your business, dear Father, not mine. And, incidentally, keep away from His Royal Highness, Prince Souphan, who is seated beside you tonight, because he is a good Buddhist, and he probably wants to remain that way."

Dooley saw the many distinguished physicians and medical educators in his audience, and couldn't resist the temptation to take a poke at the specialists. He told his favorite story about having to work with the witch doctors in Laos. "If they want to, these witch doctors can defeat everything you are trying to do in the way of providing medical care. The people in my village believe in witch doctors, just as the people of Laos have believed in them for a thousand or more years. No matter how much penicillin or other antibiotics you may shoot into a sick child, the witch doctor can defeat your purpose by later smearing the child's wound with some strange mixture of beetle juice and cow dung and things like that. So dealing with the witch doctors becomes a matter of 'if you can't lick them, join them.'

"Instead of antagonizing the witch doctors, you have to treat them as equals, or at least pretend to. You let the witch doctor sit down with you beside the sick child and you say: 'Now, this looks to me like a staphylococcus infection, and it may well develop into osteomyelitis.' While the witch doctor thinks that over, you give the kid a shot of an antibiotic. Then the witch doctor mumbles back to you something that is just as noncommittal and meaningless as the opinion you might get from any specialist right here in St. Louis. [Loud laughter and applause] Ah, thank you, doctors! We must have a few general practitioners in the house!

"Well, doctors, let me finish my story. Let's get back to the case where we had the witch doctor sit in as consultant. The next day everybody's happy. The baby is well and laughing again, so the parents are happy. The witch doctor who sat in as consultant is happy, because he is convinced that the cure resulted from his incantations and not from the needle I jabbed in the baby's behind. And I'm pretty happy myself, because the witch doctor did no harm to the patient and because everything came out so well.

"But when the grateful parents hand me two coconuts as my fee, I must be careful to give one coconut to the witch doctor in payment for his services. You can't do that here in America, because the A.M.A. would call it splitting fees!"

That evening the Jaycees raised more than $18,000 for the airplane Dooley had always wanted, so he was in high spirits at the reception which followed the banquet. He already had picked out the plane—a twin-engine Piper Apache; and he had lined up a pilot, Jerry Euster, who had flown in the Far East for CAT (Civil Air Transport), which Dooley described as the "lineal descendant of Claire Chennault's Flying Tigers."

"You have no idea how much this plane is going to mean to me," he said. "It will enable me to cover a lot more territory in a lot less time. It will enable me to get our new hospital started in Ban Houei Sai, and to give a lot more of my time to new Medico projects in South Vietnam, Cambodia and other places."

It was long after midnight when they escorted Prince Souphan, Dr. Thongphet and Mr. Pradith to their suite of rooms in the Jefferson Hotel. Then Bob Copenhaver and Crawford King, an old family friend, agreed that it was well past bedtime. But Tom Dooley, as he had said several times, was getting tired of fund raising and speech making. "Boy, how I'd love to sneak away, and have a beer, and put my feet up or maybe go to a movie or something like that. Hell, do you realize I've only seen one movie in all the four months I've been in America?"

Now he insisted upon going over to the Chase Club where the big attraction was the Kingston Trio, the California ex-college boys (Dave Guard, Bob Shane, and Nick Reynolds )who had made a great hit of the ballad "Hang Down Your Head, Tom Dooley" (no relation to Dr. Tom). Many people, including Tom's mother, despised the song because of the association of names. But Dr. Tom Dooley insisted that it was good fun as well as good music, and he was sure that the song's popularity also made people think of him, and therefore in some way benefited Medico.

"We caught the Kingston Trio's last performance of the evening," says Bob Copenhaver. "Then the three boys came over to our table and joined us for a drink. Of course, Tom started telling them about his work in Laos and how he had taught more than 500 'snotty-nosed kids' in his village to sing 'Hang Down Your Head, Tom Dooley.' This was probably an exaggeration, but it served its purpose, and Tom quickly got to the point.

"'Listen,' he told the boys, 'right at this moment we've got a royal prince of Laos and two of his friends over in the Jefferson Hotel. They've come all the way to St. Louis just to be guests at this big dinner in my honor tonight, and I am pretty sure they haven't had much fun. So, how about doing me a favor? Bring your stuff over to their hotel and put on a real good act for them.'"

Thus, sometime after three in the morning, Dooley, Copenhaver, Crawford King and the Kingston Trio, carrying their instruments, piled into taxicabs and headed for the Jefferson Hotel. For the next two hours, in the Royal Suite, the Kingston Trio played and sang Calypso songs and folk music, while the young pajama-clad prince, grinning from ear to ear, stamped out the beat with his bare feet. Then Bob Copenhaver and Tom taught the Trio a ballad they had improvised that evening, "I Was a Cooley for Dooley," to the tune of "Hang Down Your Head."

"Sure, Dooley himself seemed to be having a good time, and I was glad of it," says Bob Copenhaver. "But I knew he was just doing it to liven up the visit for his distinguished guests. Later, when we were on the way to our own hotel, he said to me, 'Remind me to drop a hint to the prince that he ought to do something for the Kingston Trio. He might send them an elephant or something.'"


Bob Copenhaver headed home, a weary but wiser man, ten pounds lighter than when he last weighed himself in Holyoke, Massachusetts. They had covered 37 cities, made 49 speeches, and had raised nearly a million dollars for Medico's operating fund. Bob Copenhaver didn't realize it at the time, but he would

be back on "active duty" on three more occasions—
once again as a "Cooley for Dooley," once as an observer in Southeast Asia, and on one final mission that
would scar his memory for the rest of his life.

Dooley left for Laos on December 16, with brief
stopovers in London, Paris, Rome, Tehran, Delhi,
and Bangkok. When he landed in London there were
a number of photographers and reporters waiting at
the airport. He emerged from the plane sleepless, di-
sheveled, needing a shave, and looking sicker than he
actually was.

Someone asked him how he felt. Characteristically,
Dooley forgot all Bob Copenhaver had said about flippancy with the press.

"I feel like hell!" he snapped. "I feel about sixty
years old!"

That remark, supported by his appearance, touched
off a small journalistic brushfire. The news was cabled
back to the United States that Dr. Tom Dooley was
dying. He was immediately deluged by cables and
phone calls and had to take refuge in Mark Twain's
famous retort that the reports of his death had been
greatly exaggerated.

Later, from Bangkok, Tom wrote a contrite letter
to Bob Copenhaver promising to be more careful in
the future. He also wrote "En route I snuck off to
Lourdes for a few hours. . . . Don't know how much
good it will do, but one never can tell. Personally, I

believe that if Someone is going to work a miracle for Dooley, it will not be dependent on whether or not Dooley went to Lourdes."


*December 19.* The temperature in Bangkok was a sizzling 110 degrees when Dooley's plane landed at the Don Muang airport. He emerged from the airplane rumpled, sweaty, but exhilarated. He was now within striking distance of what he always called "my high valley"—Muong Sing. His spirits soared when, as he entered the terminal building, he was recognized and greeted on all sides by customs officers, porters and airline employees. The woman at the newsstand greeted him heartily: "Welcome back, Dr. Dooley. How do you feel?"

This time there was none of the glumness or flippancy that had marred the London stopover. Everyone said he looked wonderful, so Dooley answered: "I *feel* wonderful. I've had a wonderful trip over and now I'm ready and rarin' to go!"

He spent three nights in Bangkok and arrived in Vientiane, capital of Laos, on December 22. There he heard rumors that the government of Prime Minister Phoui Sananikone was in trouble. Dooley dismissed the rumors as unimportant—"Just another case of the youngsters trying to kick out the oldsters"—and insisted that he could get along with a new regime as well as the old.

He learned that a number of reporters, including Jim Lucas of the Scripps-Howard newspapers, were flying up to Muong Sing to cover his homecoming. He explained that he had a few days of business to transact in Vientiane, but gave Jim Lucas a letter to Earl Rhine and Dwight Davis. He promised them he would arrive on Christmas morning, and gave detailed instructions for his own reception. He wanted the village women to butcher and barbecue two water buffalo. He wanted a floral arch erected at the little airport. He told Dwight to arrange to have school dismissed and the children assembled at the airport. Finally, he wanted the soldiers of Muong Sing's garrison lined up as a guard of honor.

"When the newspapermen heard of this they said it was typical of Tom Dooley, the egotist and show-off," says Dwight Davis. "But it wasn't like Tom at all. First of all, Tom knew that it is impossible to kill, dress and barbecue a buffalo on twenty-four hours notice. Secondly, he knew better than anyone that closing school, erecting a floral arch, and turning out the troops were honors rated by no one less than the King himself.

"Moreover, he knew that the political situation at the moment was pretty touchy, and that this was no time to stage a big Dooley celebration upon the China border where the Commies were already calling him a 'Paper Tiger' and using him to stir up anti-American sentiment.

"We never could figure out that letter, so we just dismissed it as one of Tom's rather wild gags."

On Christmas morning, in Vientiane, 400 pounds of gaily wrapped presents were loaded aboard a plane borrowed from the Lao government. Dooley climbed aboard, and the pilot took off. When they reached Muong Sing around noontime the high valley was completely "socked in" with heavy fog. After circling for about an hour the pilot turned back and landed at Luang Prabang, the old capital, halfway between Vientiane and Muong Sing. For a couple of hours they sat on the Luang Prabang airstrip under a blazing tropical sun. At 3:00 P.M. they took off again and this time found Muong Sing clear.

They circled over the hospital several times, and saw the people running from the houses, then they touched down on the little landing strip. The old jeep coughed up the trail bearing Earl Rhine, Dwight Davis and several of the newsmen. The mayor, governor and the chief of police appeared followed by a crowd of villagers. Although there was no floral arch or guard of honor, Tom Dooley received a wonderful welcome home.

"Everything is just the same as I left it," he reported to Medico, "except that the boys have given the buildings a new paint job and Earl has built a large garden, nearly half the size of a football field, on one side of the hospital. . . . Chai and Sai and Oy and the others

44

are still here—all except La who has been drafted into the army. There are 26 patients in the ward, and the clinic looks neat and clean—everything shipshape. The boys have done a magnificent job. . . ."

Earl Rhine and Dwight Davis had not seen Dooley since the preceding August when an embassy plane had picked him up on the Muong Sing airstrip to take him on the first leg of the long journey home for the cancer operation.

"Since he left we had just been sweating it out, hoping and praying," says Earl Rhine. "But here he was, back again on Christmas Day, the same old Doc, looking just wonderful. He was thinner, perhaps, but his color was good and he was in the best of spirits. But you could tell that he was having trouble with that right arm from the way he held it. We didn't think much about that at the time."

That night there was a big Christmas dinner (roasted chicken, no water buffalo) for Dooley's staff and guests. Then Tom began passing out the presents he had brought all the way from the United States— sweaters for the girls, bright colored shirts for Sai, Oy and Chai, pencils, knives, pocket combs, nail files for the Lao students. For the Lao chief nurse, Dooley had bought a fine stethoscope on which the nurse's name (in Lao) was spelled out in tiny colored beads. There was also an extra present for Chai, a woolen jacket, "because Chai is always the first one up every morn-

45

ing, and when it's cold his chattering teeth disturb the neighbors."

Earl Rhine reports: "There never was anything we could get for Doc—no presents we could ever give him. And, anyhow, Muong Sing is not a place where you can do much Christmas shopping. But Dwight had a bright idea for a Christmas present for Dooley which we could make ourselves. Doc always got great joy and relaxation out of playing our zinc-lined piano. But there was a dip in the floor right where his heel rested when he had his foot on the pedal. He always complained about it, and threatened to have it fixed, but he never did anything about it. So Dwight and I made a special foot-rest for him, wrapped it up as best we could, and enclosed a note which read something like this:

'Dear Friend:
    'Congratulations! You have just become the proud owner of a model 83 X "Little Jim Dandy Piano Foot-Rest."
    'The Little Jim Dandy is designed especially for the discriminating pianist who prefers a concert-quality foot-rest to the ordinary type.
    'The Little Jim Dandy is handcrafted by clannish tribesmen high in the mist-shrouded mountains of northern Laos. Only the finest materials are used in the manufacture of this product. The Little Jim Dandy is guaranteed for many years of service, and if it breaks down it will be replaced immediately without charge.
    'Hoping that this gift will make your piano playing

more comfortable in the future, we wish you a Merry Christmas and a Happy New Year.

> '(Signed) Dwight W. Davis, President
> Earl R. Rhine, President
> Little Jim Dandy Company
> Main Office: Muong Sing, Laos'"

Dooley had brought with him about 160 individually wrapped gifts for the kids of Muong Sing, many of whom had been milling around in the yard all during dinner, some crowded on the porch with their noses pressed against the screens. Earl and Dwight lined them up in the yard, and one by one they filed into the dining room and received their gifts. This caused a great deal of laughter, because each gift—a game, a bag of marbles, or a box of modeling clay—had to be explained to a child who had never seen anything like it before. Most of Dooley's explanations ended with the admonition, "DON'T EAT!"

"Lord have mercy on us," he said when it was all over. "We'll probably be digging marbles and pumping modeling clay out of those kids all next week!"

He spent the next few days working in the clinic, presiding over morning sick call, doing what minor surgery his sore right arm permitted. In the early evenings he strolled around Muong Sing visiting patients and seeing old friends. Then, into the early hours of the next morning, he dictated on SoundScriber discs after-

47

thoughts which he hoped his publisher might be able to insert somehow in the already completed book.

*December 28-31.* The political storm clouds had been gathering over Laos almost since the day of Dooley's arrival; and, despite his offhand reference to the squabble between the "youngsters and the oldsters," he was worried by what was going on. His determination to stand clear of Lao domestic politics was sincere, and his conviction that he could get along with one government as well as with another was genuine. Yet there were aspects of the current situation which he didn't like. So, on December 28, he flew to Vientiane "to do some political fence-mending and assess Medico's fortunes."

Early in December, Premier Phoui Sananikone had proposed to extend the expiration date of December 25, when the National Assembly of Laos was scheduled to leave office, to April 1960. This proposal was opposed by Foreign Minister Khamphan Panya and other members of the rival CDIN party (the "young reformers") who favored a more vigorous anti-communist and anti-corruption policy than Sananikone and the majority RPL party has pursued. As a result Khamphan and several other cabinet ministers who supported him were dismissed by Phoui Sananikone on December 15.

During the Christmas holidays, while Dooley was in

Muong Sing, Premier Sananikone's palace was surrounded by tanks and armored cars and a coup d'etat was staged by a Royal Lao Army group led by General Phoumi Nosavan. Negotiations for a peaceful settlement of the squabble continued for several days between the generals and the Sananikone government. Then, on December 29, Dooley's good friend, Deputy Premier Katay Don Sasorith ("the only man Sananikone could rely upon when dealing with the Army") died suddenly of a coronary embolism.

Thereafter things moved swiftly to a climax. On December 30, while Dooley was in Bangkok, Lao troops seized all government buildings, communications centers, airport and power plant. Sananikone sent his resignation to the King, who accepted it and appointed a provisional government headed by General Phoumi Nosavan.

Dooley's attitude was a saddened but hopeful one of "let's wait and see." Much would depend upon the national elections set for April 1960.

He spent New Year's Eve alone, dictating letters in his room in the Erawan Hotel—"this year, strangely enough, I haven't the slightest desire to 'ring out the old, ring in the new.'"

It was long after midnight when he gathered the discs to be airmailed to Teresa Gallagher in New York. In addition to the numerous thank-you notes to people who had befriended him and made contributions to Medico during his U.S. lecture tour, there were some personal letters that carried vague notes of sadness and nostalgia which some recipients failed to recognize until many months later.

He acknowledged a letter from his brother, Malcolm Dooley, who had sent a clipping of the December Gallup Poll naming Tom Dooley one of the ten "World's Most Admired Men" along with such leaders as Eisenhower, Churchill and Pope John XXIII. "This staggers me, and frightens me. They keep pushing me higher and higher. When will people begin to think of Medico, and not of Tom Dooley? How many people know—or care—who started the Red Cross, and yet isn't the Red Cross itself all that really matters?"

He wrote a long letter to Dr. Peter Comanduras, Director General of Medico: "It is 9:45 P.M. on New Year's Eve. First, my very sincere thanks, Peter, for your friendship, for your devotion, for your love for a guy named Dooley. And thanks, most of all, for being Peter Comanduras, the head of Medico. We need you, Peter, very, very much. . . .

"I feel okay, but I know I'm not the same Dooley I was a year ago. I definitely lack the old get-up-and-go I used to have. . . . It's obvious to me now, Peter, that you must find a young doctor to replace me at Muong Sing. . . . I am planning this with one awful thought in mind—that I may not be able to return to Laos after my scheduled check-up in May. If I can—fine! If I cannot, then Medico in Laos must be cared for. . . . Medico must always be a living, thriving thing for ever and ever. . . ."

# PART TWO

# 1960:

# WINTER

With the beginning of the new year, Tom Dooley's impatience, and his frequently ill-tempered drive, became obvious to everyone who saw him. For a week or more he worried and fumed in Bangkok over the long-delayed arrival of pilot Jerry Euster and the Piper Apache. Jerry Euster had reported from St. Louis on December 19, and again from Madrid on December 22. Now, more than two weeks later, the plane was long overdue.

On the morning of January 8, Dooley was in the lobby of the Erawan Hotel when Jerry Euster walked through the door. He had been held over in Madrid and Istanbul by governmental red tape, and again in Karachi by bad weather. He actually had been flying a dangerously over-loaded airplane. Tom Dooley's peremptory orders as to what cargo the Apache was to bring from the States had been issued without any knowledge of the standard rules of weight-and-loading, and only Jerry's skillful flying had brought the airplane safely over its long journey. Meanwhile,

Euster had been reporting regularly, according to orders, to Dooley's headquarters in Muong Sing, via Vientiane, when Dooley was in Bangkok.

They flew to Vientiane on January 9, went through the red tape of registering the plane with the Lao authorities, and spent the night at the home of Dooley's long-time friends, Hank and Annie Miller. Two new members of the Muong Sing team, Tom Kirby and Alan Rommel, were at the Millers' house waiting for them. The next morning, January 10, the foursome took off for Muong Sing.

Dooley's impatience subsided momentarily, and he gloated over the airplane like a small boy with a new toy. "What do you know! Jerry flew us from Vientiane in an hour and fifty-five minutes," he exclaimed when they landed. "Even the commercial planes take longer than that!"

*January 11-31.* Dooley spent the rest of the month at Muong Sing, working in the hospital with Earl, Dwight and the Lao nurses, and indoctrinating the new corpsmen, Tom Kirby and Alan Rommel. It was during this period that Earl and Dwight first became aware of Dooley's strange new sense of urgency.

"We could see that Doc was driving himself too hard," says Earl Rhine, "and we wondered and talked about it. We weren't sure, at first, whether this was because he was afraid his condition might get worse,

54

or whether he just wanted to get things running smoothly at Muong Sing so that he would be free to do other things. We knew about the plan to start a new hospital over in Ban Houei Sai. He also had told us that early in February he planned to fly up to northern Burma to see Dr. Gordon Seagrave, and right after that he wanted to spend some time with Dr. Manny Voulgaropoulos in the Medico hospital at Kratie, Cambodia.

"But Dwight and I were convinced that Doc was really pushing against time. He had always been a 'young man in a hurry' ever since we'd known him, but somehow this was different. He was also bombarding New York with letters and cables about the doctor who was supposed to replace him at Muong Sing, and he was angry because New York was so slow about finding the right man."

Earl and Dwight had been in Muong Sing since the hospital was opened in the fall of 1958. Their 18 month "tour of duty" with Dooley would end in March, and they were already planning their departure. Tom Kirby, 22, and Alan Rommel, 27, their replacements, were seeing Muong Sing—and Dr. Tom Dooley in action—for the first time.

Tall, husky, crew-cut Alan Rommel first heard of Dr. Dooley when, on his way to Laos for the first time, Dooley stopped off in Rommel's hometown, Evansville, Indiana, to visit the Mead-Johnson Pharmaceutical Company, which had donated a large supply of drugs for the proposed hospitals. Rommel tells how he became interested in Dr. Dooley's work:

There was a lot about Dooley in the local papers. After that, while I was a medical aide in the Army during 1956-58, I followed his career closely through his books and articles. But it wasn't until August 1959, when he came home for the cancer operation, that I began to think seriously about applying for a place on one of his teams.

I was then 27 years old, single, with no strings attached, and I thought that my Army experience might qualify me for a job as corpsman. However, I didn't have Medico's New York address at the time, so I didn't do anything about it. But about a month later, while I was attending a Russian language class in the evening, the instructor happened to mention that Dr. Tom Dooley was in Evansville, and that a reception for him was to be given the next day. That's where I met him the first time. I spoke to him for only a few minutes, and gave him a written résumé of my experience, which he folded and placed in his pocket.

Two weeks later I got a letter from him asking me to come to St. Louis for a personal interview. There I was interviewed by a doctor friend of Tom Dooley's, and then by Bob Copenhaver. Apparently, they turned in favorable reports, because when I saw Dr. Dooley later in the day, he merely said: "You're hired and you are going to Laos next week."

That rather took my breath away, but I soon learned that it was typically Dooley. He seemed to have innate judgment of people. He didn't probe very deeply himself; he relied on the opinions of other people he trusted. I think he realized that most people who wanted to work for Medico had pretty good reasons for their decision. Motivation, experience and character carried a lot of weight with him.

I arrived in Muong Sing in January 1960. Because of my previous medical corps training, I was assigned to the operating room, and to taking care of the patients in the ward—feeding them, administering drugs, taking temperatures, etc. Tom Kirby, who arrived about the same time, had not had any previous medical training. But he did speak French fluently, so Dr. Dooley turned over to him most of the administrative work, although Tom Kirby gradually assumed some medical chores. Incidentally, all of us had to pitch in and do manual labor occasionally. You have to be a jack-of-all-trades in a place like Muong Sing.

I soon learned how Dooley got his reputation of being a hard man to work for. He was neither a tyrant nor a prima donna. But he was a perfectionist wherever the hospital, clinic and patients were concerned. He put a lot of himself into everything he did, and he expected everyone associated with him, whether they were Americans or Lao, to do the same. He did have an Irish temper, but the only times I saw it flare up was when someone did a careless or stupid thing or sloppy job.

I think the first thing I observed in Muong Sing was the people's absolute faith and confidence in Dr. Dooley. They literally worshipped him. The children, no matter how sick they were, never bawled or complained when the parents brought them to see the doctor. The *Thanh Mo America* was a god to them, and a very gentle and understanding one. Many older women frequently came to the clinic merely to be checked over. Like women in America, they saw the doctor and went away feeling better, whether or not there was anything wrong with them in the first place. I remember mentioning this to Dr. Dooley several times. He merely laughed and made some wisecrack about "psychosomatic medicine."

The thing that bothered me most was his repeated reference to the kind of "nineteenth century medicine" that he was practicing. I objected particularly when he made that statement to Americans, and particularly to American newspapermen. He was really a very good doctor, and would rank with the best young general practitioners anywhere in the United States. He was using the latest antibiotic drugs and applying the latest surgical techniques. He was practicing a better kind of medicine than the "twentieth century" medicine that was practiced in the U.S. before World War II. Actually, most of the patients in the Muong Sing Clinic received the same medication that is prescribed today by most Park Avenue physicians.

Of course, the idea Dr. Dooley was trying to get across to the American public was that you don't need white-tile operating rooms, stainless steel equipment, and air-conditioning in order to treat sick people living in the mud-huts of Asia. We didn't have any fancy stuff in Muong. We couldn't afford it. And if we waited until we could afford it, the miserable people in Muong Sing would have gone without any medical assistance at all. What we had was primitive but adequate. Our operating room may not have been as aseptic and spotless as those in the United States, but we didn't have any infections either. We had to improvise, but we got by pretty well.

I was surprised by the daily case-load; it was often larger than you would get in the clinic of a good-size American hospital. The number of patients per day would vary. On a very bad day, rainy day, we might have only 20-25 patients. However, on a nice day we might get up to 150 or 160 in the morning when we had out-patient clinic. Those who were well enough to receive medication and go back to their village were treated right there. Those who had to come back every day received a piece of paper and were told to return. They'd come back, present the paper, and we'd know what to do for them. Those who were sick enough to be hospitalized we'd put into the wards.

We could accommodate up to 32 people in a ward. We had another bamboo hut where we could put a few more people. Also, one of our coolies had a little house with mud walls where a few patients from his village could stay. So we could accommodate 40-50 people. Not all of them would be patients, however, because often a patient would come to the hospital with his mother, father, children, grandparents, aunts, and uncles! In one room you might have ten people, but only two would be patients. The rest would be relatives. The relatives would look after the patients and cook their food. If something happened they could run over to the house and tell us.

Unless a person had a particular type of illness where diet was important, we let them eat their native food. If they didn't have food, they could come to our house. But most of them preferred their own food. We never had to worry about that.

All patients who were hospitalized got a high-protein-and-vitamin food supplement which we mixed with water. It looked like milk and they liked it very much. While they were recuperating or hospitalized they got a very good diet.

Alan Rommel soon became accustomed to the lonely life in isolated Muong Sing. "The days were long, and we were all dog-tired by nightfall. We would light the kerosene lamps, have dinner, and then sit around reading, talking, or writing letters. We took turns answering the night calls and the emergencies that were always popping up. When Dr. Dooley's arm wasn't bothering him too much, he would play the piano. We also had a battery-operated record player, and a radio on which we could pick up the Voice of America, the BBC and some other stations. But the evenings were rather lonely. I learned to go to bed and get to sleep early. After that first month I even got accustomed to the sound of Dooley's voice dictating into that machine all night long."

*February 1-4.* On the morning of February 1, the Muong Sing hospital was astir even earlier than usual with preparations for the flight to north Burma. Jerry Euster went down at the landing strip shortly after dawn to pre-flight the airplane, happy over the prospect of doing more than shuttling supplies between Muong Sing and Vientiane. ("Jerry Euster isn't quite accustomed yet to the slow-moving ways of our Lao friends," Dooley had written. "When he tells them to do something, and they look at him with that languid *bau pinh yanh* [which Dooley translated as 'what-the-hell, why hurry?'] attitude, I am always afraid Jerry is going to hit them on the head. However, he is learning fast and, he is really a wonderful pilot. His pinpoint navigation is really something to behold, and I have a sense of complete security when I am in the air with him.")

Dooley presided at sick call that morning, and with his staff handled over 100 patients. It was 11 A.M. when he climbed aboard the plane, followed by Dwight and Earl. Jerry Euster already had the engines turning over.

Tom Dooley's admiration for Dr. Gordon Seagrave, the famous Burma surgeon, was surpassed only by his reverence for Dr. Albert Schweitzer. During the preceding year, Medico had given Dr. Seagrave's hospital in Namkhan, north of Lashio, Burma, about $100,000 worth of drugs and equipment, plus several thousand dollars in cash. Tom Dooley had never met Dr. Seagrave, but he felt a strong spiritual kinship with this man who had spent nearly forty years serving the sick people of Asia.

The Seagrave hospital in northern Burma lies northwest of Muong Sing in northern Laos, little more than an hour away as the crow (or a Piper Apache) flies. But both villages are dangerously close to the border of Red China, and a great many international regulations made the direct flight impossible. Jerry planned

61

to fly south to Vientiane, make a quick stopover for luncheon and refueling, and then fly to Bangkok and stop there overnight to obtain visas and the necessary permits from the Burmese Embassy.

On the morning of Tuesday, February 2, they took off from Bangkok and landed at Rangoon late that night. The next morning Dooley presented himself to Mr. James Barrington (a Burmese), secretary of state of the Union of Burma, and later paid a courtesy call on General Ne Win, then the prime minister. Both did their best to dissuade him from attempting the hazardous flight to the north. They warned him that in addition to the *dacoits,* the Burmese bandits and murderers celebrated by Rudyard Kipling, the northern frontier was now seething with Burmese insurgents and Communist infiltrators from Red China.

"Of course, Dr. Dooley wasn't easily dissuaded by that kind of argument," says Earl Rhine. "He had heard it every time he attempted to arrange field trips into the interior of Laos. Now, it seemed to me, he was using the same old counter-arguments to get us up into northern Burma."

Tom Dooley, the veteran diplomat, finally wangled permission for the Piper Apache to fly north to Lashio, and persuaded the prime minister to telegraph orders for the garrison at Lashio to provide Dooley's party with jeeps and armed guards for the four-hour trip to Dr. Seagrave's hospital at Namkhan.

They took off that afternoon, and three and a half

hours later made a scheduled stopover at Mandalay, although Jerry Euster insisted that he had fuel enough to make Lashio before nightfall. When they landed in Mandalay, Dooley realized that it was a mistake. There was a large group of Burmese officials on hand to greet them. When the amenities were over, they gave Dooley the bad news. General Ne Win had countermanded his original orders to allow the plane to proceed to Lashio. The airport officials had orders to instruct pilot Euster to fly directly back to Rangoon.

Dooley surprised everyone by taking this setback philosophically. They flew back to Rangoon, and Dooley spent the next morning listening to Burmese regrets and apologies. He made the best of a bad situation by educating the top Burmese officials on the aims and purposes of Medico, paving the way for the establishment of a Medico hospital in Burma.

Before they departed, Dooley paid a diplomatic call on the prime minister, and General Ne Win held out a vague promise that within a few weeks, when the national elections were over, things might quiet down in the north. Then Dr. Dooley and his party might be permitted to fly to Lashio. Dooley never did meet Dr. Gordon Seagrave face to face.

*February* 5. On the return flight to Bangkok, Dooley decided that they would stop over in Vientiane for two days, transact some business in the capital, and then fly over to Cambodia for his long-scheduled conference with Dr. Manny Voulgaropoulos.

During the preceding eighteen months, young Dr. Voulgaropoulos had made a notable success of the Medico hospital in the little city of Kratie in southern Cambodia. The hospital was larger than Dooley's, and better equipped; because of the proximity to the city of Kratie, it even had the benefits of electricity and running water.

Dooley had a genuine affection for Dr. Voulgaropoulos and his wife, Rose. He admired Manny, not only as a doctor but as a creative administrator. The success of the Kratie hospital had convinced the Cambodian government of the integrity and importance of the Medico idea, and time was ripe for an expansion of Medico's activities in the country. Dooley was satisfied that Manny Voulgaropoulos had some sound ideas about what shape the developments should take.

On the morning of February 8, while Jerry Euster filed his flight plan, Dooley stopped in the airport and sent a wire to Mrs. John W. McCarthy, Jr. in Phnom Penh. MEET ME AT PHNOM PENH AIRPORT NOON TODAY. LOVE, TOM DOOLEY.


Patricia (Pat) McCarthy, a pretty girl with blondish hair and a genuine "school-girl complexion," received the wire that morning in the small American-built apartment in Phnom Penh which she occupied with her husband, John, who is attached to the U.S. Operations Mission to Cambodia. There was barely time to finish what she was doing, dress, and drive to the airport to meet Dooley's plane at noon.

Pat Christensen and John McCarthy, both from La Porte, Indiana, had met Tom Dooley in 1942, when all three of them were only sixteen years old. Pat McCarthy writes:

> Tom was a student at Notre Dame then, but he often spent his weekends in La Porte. He was tall and slender, with dark wavy hair, cool blue eyes and devastating lashes. He won the heart of every girl present on that quiet Sunday afternoon when we met him. The boys, needless to say, were less than charmed by him!
>
> He played the piano marvelously, with six or eight of the girls hanging on every note. He could jitterbug like a professional, and he had an easy way of flipping his partner over his back—something we hadn't seen done anywhere but in the movies.
>
> He affected a very sophisticated, worldly manner, and I remember how he shocked us all by saying that the loveliest perfume in the world was the fragrance of woman fresh from her bath. We were just sixteen, remember! We also found it exciting when he talked of his plans to be a 'society doctor' and specialize in obstetrics. If anyone had told us then that Tom would one day devote his life to the sick people in the under-developed nations of Southeast Asia, I am sure we all would have laughed out loud.
>
> But those lazy, fun-filled Sunday afternoons in La Porte ended all too soon. Most of the boys went into the

Army, Navy or the Air Force. Tom joined the Navy. We didn't see him again for fifteen years.

When John and I arrived in Cambodia in 1956, we knew Tom Dooley was in the Far East. We had read *Deliver Us From Evil,* and we hoped to see him out here. But Laos is a long way from Cambodia, and it was many months before we met him.

Then, on a Tuesday morning in 1957, I went to the embassy residence for our regular weekly "sewing-coffee." We were knee-deep in little dresses and things for the orphans, when Tom walked in. Most of the women shrieked with delight, for Tom Dooley was now rather famous. I sat stunned. Even knowing that I would see him one day hadn't lessened the surprise. He had launched into a talk about his work, and then he looked over and saw me. He stopped, walked over and kissed me, then he turned to Mrs. Strom, the Ambassador's wife, and said, "Excuse me, but this is my old sweetheart." I never was his sweetheart, of course, but his saying so raised my standing in that room by twenty points!

When he joined us for dinner that night, he discovered that I was collecting opium weights—little weights shaped like animals, which the dealers in the old days used for weighing the raw opium. He said he might be able to get me a few more because they were still used in Laos. He left for Muong Sing the next day, and it was many months before we saw him again.

But he didn't forget the opium weights. A few weeks later I opened the door and Dwight Davis, a young man I'd never seen before, asked me if I was Mrs. John McCarthy. When I said yes and invited him in, he began rummaging through his pockets and produced a number of opium weights. He said, "I have a message from Dr. Dooley. . . . He says that these are all for you. He also said to tell you he still has a very rare set of seven weights, all elephants, but he is saving them for some girl who isn't married!"

The next time Tom came to Phnom Penh was late in 1958 to meet his new Cambodian team and open the hospital at Kratie. Everyone was wonderful to them, and they were invited to lunch and dinner, and treated royally. That was the first time, I think, that a Dooley team was really well received by the American community anywhere in Southeast Asia. Of course, Ambassador and Mrs. Strom set the standard, by welcoming Dr. Dooley, and the other Americans followed. But not all, I might add. There were some who considered Tom Dooley an arrogant upstart. Some had been in Saigon when Tom worked to save the Vietnamese refugees in the north, and he had tramped on too many official toes in order to get what he wanted for his projects. But it was amazing how these dissenting voices died down or changed tune as his fame grew.

There were many whirlwind visits during the next few months. The one we remember most was when he arrived late one afternoon in 1959 en route to Laos. Tom walked in, drank about two quarts of coffee, but wouldn't eat a thing. He said he thought he might be coming down with malaria. He looked terrible. My husband said, "Tom, you look like hell. I think there's something seriously wrong. Why don't you stay here for a few days and get some rest?" But Tom said he had to get back to Muong Sing and left in the morning. The next week we had a wire: YOU MUST BE CLAIRVOYANTS. AM ON MY WAY TO THE STATES FOR DIAGNOSIS AND TREAT-

MENT. Then we heard about the cancer operation in New York.

These were Pat McCarthy's thoughts and memories as she waited at the Phnom Penh airport that day in February 1960. The Piper Apache landed and Tom stepped out, followed by Earl Rhine and Jerry Euster. Pat continues her story:

Now he was back, this time in his own plane. What a blessing that little plane was to him. Never could he have done so much, in the little time he had left, without it!

We all came home for lunch. It was then that I realized how ill Tom was. His color was good, and he was in high spirits. But he was so thin! And when I saw that he had to use both hands to raise his coffee cup—somehow, that really tore my heart out. He had to see Rose and Manny Voulgaropoulos that afternoon, and he persuaded me to come along, promising that we would be back in Phnom Penh in time for dinner. So we flew to Kratie after lunch.

On the way we read the proofs of his last book, *The Night They Burned the Mountain.* As he finished each galley sheet, he would hand it to me to read. At one point I reached for the next sheet and found him staring out at the clouds, lines deeply etched on his face and pain in his eyes. At that moment, all the happy, confident things he had been telling me about the great strides being made in cancer research and his chance of recovery went right out the window. I had a hard time holding back the tears.

At Kratie, Tom made a quick inspection of the hospital and had a brief conference with Dr. Manny while Rose Voulgaropoulos entertained the others. Rose was expecting a baby in June, and arrangements had been made for the confinement in the Saigon Hospital, where an old friend and classmate of Manny's was serving as obstetrician.

When Tom returned to the living room he had a worried frown on his face. He and Manny had lots of things to discuss, he said, and since it was nearly four o'clock and the little Kratie airport closed at sundown, Rose and Manny would fly back with them to Phnom Penh and spend the night with the McCarthys. Thus, everyone could have a nice visit, and he and Manny would have plenty of time to talk.

Dr. Voulgaropoulos and the Kratie Hospital were having trouble. Relations with the Cambodian government couldn't have been better, and the Kratie team was working smoothly. But Manny's communications with Medico's New York office had broken down completely. Particularly during the five months since Dooley returned to America for his operations, Manny's reports and requisitions had gone unanswered. There was one desperate period when his supply of essential drugs was completely exhausted. Medical services at the Kratie hospital came to a standstill. Seriously ill patients were being neglected or given make-shift treatment, which distressed conscientious young Dr. Voulgaropoulos. He also felt that there might be real trouble if the actual condition became known to the Cambodian government.

"This was in no way Dr. Dooley's fault," Manny says. "Each hospital is autonomous and deals directly with New York. My hospital in Kratie, for example, had the same status as Tom's hospital in Muong Sing. Of course, if he had been in Muong Sing at the time, I could have appealed to him for help and he would have done something to correct this situation. But he wasn't in Muong Sing, he was thousands of miles away, so all I could do was to continue bombarding New York with complaints and urgent appeals. I never got an answer.

"My desperate situation was solved by sheer good luck. There was a young Chinese in Cambodia who represented several American drug companies. Somehow he got in wrong with the Cambodian government and was ordered to leave the country. He was stuck with an inventory of pharmaceuticals worth about $60,000. It was cheaper to leave them there than ship them to some other country. So, being aware of my problem, he presented the whole lot to the Kratie hospital. That's what saved the day."

Tom realized that there was a plausible explanation for Manny's difficulties. They had occurred while Medico was still functioning as a subsidiary of the International Rescue Committee and before the new independent Medico, Inc. (which still was in the organization stage), had been set up. Nevertheless, the

70

problem was serious and Tom was determined that it must not recur. He was now planning more hospitals and expanding Medico's operations in other countries, hence the lines of communication and supply would be even more important than ever. He assured Manny that the supply system would be changed. He also reminded him that such things happened even in the best-run organizations, and that the American by-word for even our most victorious military operations was often "Snafu."

They tried to forget their troubles and joined Pat, John, Rose and Jerry Euster in the McCarthys' living room. Tom Dooley put on a good show, exhibiting confidence and high spirits. Manny outlined his plans for a second Medico hospital in southern Cambodia. He also wanted to provide a pediatrics service for the several orphanages in Phnom Penh, and to arrange for visiting specialists to serve as lecturers at the Cambodian medical school. Then there was the problem of the Soviet-built hospital in Phnom Penh, which Tom Dooley and Manny both considered an exciting and challenging opportunity.

The hospital, really a small medical center, had been built by the Soviets as a dramatic counter-measure to the U.S. foreign-aid program. The central building was a 500-bed hospital, and this was surrounded by several smaller buildings for laboratories, residences, and a nurses' home. "It's really a magnificent setup,"

Dooley exclaimed. "It looks almost like the Naval Medical Institute at Bethesda, Maryland."

However, in February 1960, the spick-and-span medical center was actually a Soviet white elephant. The Cambodian Government had neither the doctors nor the funds to operate the hospital. The Soviets had offered to supply medical personnel, although this was not part of the original agreement, but the Cambodian government had politely declined the offer. Instead, the Minister of Health had quietly approached Dr. Voulgaropoulos with the suggestion that Medico might provide or arrange for an American staff.

While this sounded like a huge undertaking, probably beyond Medico's means, Manny thought it should be possible for a Medico team to staff and operate at least one of the major services, perhaps pediatrics or orthopedic surgery. He suggested that Medico might arrange for other organizations, or even the U.S. foreign-aid program, to staff the rest of the hospital. Such an arrangement, he said, would be acceptable to the Cambodian government. Tom Dooley heartily endorsed the idea.

Unhappily, no action ever was taken on the Voulgaropoulos proposal. Time dragged on and, in November 1960, the Phnom Penh Hospital was finally staffed by Soviet doctors, nurses, and technicians. Manny Voulgaropoulos says sadly: "I am still convinced that Medico, and indeed the United States, missed a golden opportunity."

"That was a crowded, but happy evening," says Pat McCarthy. "Crowded because we have only one bedroom in our little apartment, and we had six people to sleep that night. John, Tom and Jerry went upstairs and slept in the apartment that had just been vacated by one of our friends. Rose and Manny took our bedroom, and I slept across the hall with a girl who works in the embassy.

"But it was a happy evening because Tom was in fine spirits and kept everybody in a gay mood. It was the last time we saw him so relaxed. When we saw him again, many months later, he was a dying man, in agonizing pain, and yet still trying gamely to get his job done."

*February 14-16.* When they got back to Muong Sing, they found that Don Cravens and Scot Leavitt, a *Life* photographer-writer team, had taken over. Cravens and Leavitt had been assigned to do a special feature story and, as usual when publicity was at stake, Dooley cooperated fully. But, at the end of a week, he reported to New York: "Leavitt and Cravens are really nice guys, but I sure am sick and tired of them snapping pictures and asking questions every time I turn around. They have been snooping into every angle of our business, talking to all sorts of people, staging all kinds of stunts, and photographing the place inside and out from dawn

73

to midnight. . . . Well, I hope they get a good story out of it."

Many people have said that Tom Dooley was his own best press agent. The truth is that Dooley was really a babe-in-arms where publicity was concerned. He had the naïve notion that any and all publicity was good publicity so long as it mentioned Tom Dooley and Medico. Indeed, he could be emphatic and sometimes sarcastic in rejecting some proposals that seemed to emphasize Tom Dooley alone. For example, during February 1960, someone in the New York office inadvertantly mentioned in a memo to Dooley that "personal stationery" was being prepared for letters addressed to supporters and contributors. Dooley dictated a memo that made his SoundScriber crackle: "I don't—repeat *do not*—need personal stationery! Whoever thought that one up ought to go and stand in the corner. People who give us money or otherwise support us are not doing it for Tom Dooley, they are doing it for Medico. Let's never forget that. I don't care how you people in New York use my name, as long as you are sure that it helps Medico. But let's not get silly. . . ."

When dealing directly with the press, however, Dooley invarably dropped his guard. He was, as Bob Copenhaver once remarked, "as willing and as eager as a round-heeled gal in a Navy port of call." Thus, despite what he had to say about it later, during Leavitt's and Cravens' visit to Muong Sing, he proceeded to give the *Life* men "the works." He made them virtually a part of a Medico team, took them in his home and clinic, let them prowl with him through the streets and alleys of the village, and really showed them the town. For the benefit of Don Cravens' busy camera, he romped with the village children, produced some typical and some grotesque specimens of his practice—the hare-lipped boy and the bear-mauled man—and willingly assumed every extravagant or theatrical pose that was suggested to him. Says Earl Rhine: "Doc really knocked himself out on that story."

Meanwhile, he was discovering that Muong Sing was no longer the lonely and inaccessible place it was in the days before he acquired his airplane. Now he had frequent visitors and the list was growing. Paul Hellmuth, the Boston lawyer and Notre Dame trustee, arrived on February 20. A few days later Tom received a wire saying that several doctors headed by Dr. H. L. Bockus, professor of internal medicine at the University of Pennsylvania Graduate School of Medicine, would arrive early in March. He was also expecting Dr. I. S. Ravdin, surgeon-in-chief of the University of Pennsylvania Hospital. And Arthur Godfrey promised to pay a visit sometime in the near future.

Paul Hellmuth was in Muong Sing while Scot Leavitt and Don Cravens were still gathering material for the *Life* story. He watched Tom's over-eager co-operation and, privately, expressed misgivings. Tom brushed Hellmuth's fears aside: "I never worry about such things—they always take care of themselves."

*March 1-10.* Dr. H. L. Bockus and his colleagues arrived in Bangkok. Dr. Bockus reports:

We were pleasantly surprised to see at the airport, in addition to the local doctors, our friend Dr. Tom Dooley, and the pilot of his private plane, Jerry Euster. They escorted us to the hotel and there arrangements were made to fly us to Tom's hospitals in Laos. En route, we stopped off at Vientiane, Luang Prabang, and then spent several days at Muong Sing. We also flew over to Ban Houei Sai, the new project Tom was starting in Laos near the Thailand border.

We had an opportunity to observe Tom at close quarters during this trip and we were impressed by the influence which he had upon those around him. We noticed the admiration with which his young colleagues worked with him.

But we were particularly impressed by the devotion which the natives of Muong Sing had for Dr. Dooley. We were reminded very much of the story of the Pied Piper by the way the children ran toward him wherever he appeared and stuck to him like flies. I remember when our plane came down in the little meadow there must have been a hundred children running from all directions as soon as they saw his plane approaching. He played ball with them, he taught them games, and he helped the local teachers instructing them in dance steps and singing. The first thing Tom said when he stepped out of the plane was, "You are all going to see a movie tonight."

At that time I had the impression that he was pushing himself a bit hard, and I knew that he was in pain. When we were traveling around by plane, we noticed the contortions he went through trying to find a comfortable position. However, in March 1960, he was staying up until two or three in the morning, as usual, putting letters on his dictating machine.

I think Tom fully realized that his days were numbered. I remember someone asking him, while we were at Muong Sing, about whether he would be back in the States attending some meeting or other a year hence. I remember how he said, "The heart says yes, but statistics would indicate that it isn't possible." In other words, he knew he probably wouldn't last that long.

*March 12-23.* Muong Sing was operating on an unusual schedule during this period. In the mornings they would hold sick-call as usual, then, in the early afternoon, they would fly over to Ban Houei Sai where they would operate a temporary makeshift clinic and supervise construction of the new hospital.

Paul Hellmuth reports:

Tom Dooley had described a typical sick-call so many times in his books and lectures that I thought I was well prepared for what I was about to see. But, as a layman, and new to this part of the world, I was frankly appalled by the daily parade of obviously sick and diseased patients, small children, men and women, and very old people. Yet I had the opportunity of seeing each morning the very thing I had come all this way to witness—Dr. Tom Dooley in action. And that is when I discovered that there were *two* Tom Dooleys, one entirely different from the other. The first, of course, was the dramatic Tom Dooley we saw on the lecture and fund-raising circuit. The other was the quiet, patient, dedicated Dr. Tom Dooley who had very obviously endeared himself to the simple people of this primitive community.

Being a layman and something of a sightseer, at sick-call I found a place on the sidelines and tried to be as inconspicuous as possible. As a matter of fact, I was always thankful for the way Tom and the other members of the team managed to ignore me during their working day. But, gradually I began to understand the real meaning of Tom's reference to his "nineteenth century medicine" and to the fifteenth century world in which he was practicing it. Much later this enabled me to see the fallacy inherent in the *Life* story that eventually appeared. That story, in itself, was not incorrect; but the emphasis was entirely wrong. Only if you studied carefully the faces of the Lao children and adults in the photographs could you even begin to understand what Tom Dooley was really trying to do and what his ministrations meant to these people. Unfortunately you could be distracted easily from such an understanding by the more dramatic and entirely unrepresentative pictures of Tom Dooley romping with children or Tom Dooley with a pretty girl on the rear seat of his motor scooter. The latter picture, incidentally, was not taken in Muong Sing at all, but in Vientiane, the capital, when Tom Dooley was pressed into doing a sort of "good turn" by giving another American, a comparative stranger, a lift to the airport.

Paul Hellmuth watched them working at the clinic in the mornings, then he became accustomed to being hurried into the Apache in the early afternoon and being flown to Ban Houei Sai. "They've always needed us in Ban Houei Sai," said Dooley, "but when I was there last year Ban Houei Sai was a good three-day trek across the mountains and we couldn't make it very often. Now we can make it in less than forty-five minutes by plane."

Everyone who has seen Ban Houei Sai (beginning with Tom Dooley himself) exclaims at the grandeur and the natural beauty of the setting—the sweeping river, the rolling plains, and the breath-taking backdrop of high mountains. The little village lies southwest of Muong Sing on the banks of the Mekong River which forms the border between the northernmost regions of Laos and Thailand.

But Tom Dooley had not selected Ban Houei Sai for its beauty, but for the fact that the location is the perfect base from which to offer medical service to an estimated fifty thousand people—more isolated and depressed, in many respects, than those in the Muong Sing area.

By mid-March Alan Rommel and a Lao student, Kam Tung, were settled in a small hut on the river bank, not far from where the new out-patient and clinic building was already rising. The main hospital and the house that would be the living quarters of the team were also under construction on top of the hill overlooking the river. Building materials, and later all furnishings and equipment, had to be brought on the Mekong River, a convenience which also had influ-

enced Dooley's selection of the Ban Houei Sai location. "It would have been utterly impossible to bring
in everything we need—and up here we need everything—overland or by plane," Dooley reported. "The
place is completely inaccessible except by way of the
river, and of course by our little plane, which is hardly
suitable for hauling heavy construction materials."

With Alan Rommel assigned to supervise construction, Tom Kirby had been stationed in Vientiane as
procurement and logistics officer. He had already
shipped four tons of equipment from Vientiane to
Luang Prabang by commercial planes. From Luang
Prabang the stuff was then shipped by barge and river
boat to Ban Houei Sai, a five day journey. Transportation of the equipment imported from the States—operating room fixtures, surgical instruments, pharmaceuticals, furniture, and so forth—was another gigantic
problem which had thus far been worked out only on
paper. These imported things would be shipped in
bond to Bangkok, whence they would be sent north
by railway to Chiang Rai in northern Thailand, and
then overland by truck or ox cart to the Mekong River.
Months later, war and international politics were to
play havoc with this plan, and Dooley's daring solution of the problem would win him a local reputation
as the "Old Smuggler."

During the rest of March, while construction was
underway, Dooley and his team held sick-call each

afternoon on the river bank at Ban Houei Sai—much as they had in the old days when Dooley tried to treat sick people of isolated areas on his periodic river trips. But here the *Thanh Mo America* had already established his reputation, and each day the people would come down out of the mountains to Ban Houei Sai, bringing their sick and disabled with them. Tom Dooley did what he could for the ambulatory cases; a few surgical emergencies were flown over to Muong Sing; the others would have to wait for their "elective surgery" when the Ban Houei Sai hospital was fully equipped and open for business, which Tom Dooley fervently hoped would be in April or May.

Before dusk settled over the mountains the little Piper Apache would take off from the Ban Houei Sai airstrip and return to Muong Sing.

Paul Hellmuth concludes his report:

One night in March, shortly before my departure I witnessed, completely unobserved, one more little incident that helped to convince me of Tom Dooley's utter dedication to his people no matter how insignificant or hopeless they may have been.

It had been a long, hard day, particularly for a soft Westerner like myself, and when I went to bed Tom Dooley was just settling down to his night's work on his dictating machine. I was awakened from a sound sleep by voices in the living room. When I peeked out, I saw Dooley and Earl Rhine talking to a young man whom I recognized as the son of Wong, an old, emaciated Chinese who sold peanuts and Mekong whisky in a little road-level stand near the bazaar. Dooley had been treating old Wong's advanced case of tuberculosis. "He's hopeless, of course," Tom had said. "All I can do is give him palliative treatment."

Now, from what I could hear of the conversation, old Wong was having another of his coughing spasms and was hemorrhaging badly. I heard Earl say: "Doctor, I can handle this. There's no need for you to go at this hour of the morning." Dooley replied rather angrily: "Of course, I'm going! What are you guys trying to do —put me on the shelf?" Then he added, almost apologetically, as he checked through the contents of his bag, "Okay, you can come along with me if you want to."

I looked at my watch and saw that it was after 3:00 A.M. "Earl is right," I thought. "Why should Dooley waste his time on this old rascal who can't be cured and who might be better off dead?"

After Earl and Tom left, I thought of the first time I had seen old Wong, squatting beside his little stand near the bazaar. When we approached he got to his feet and greeted Tom with great deference and affection. Then he poured some stuff from a big jug into a bowl and offered it to us. Dooley said to me, "This is what they call 'Mekong whisky.' Probaby named after the dirty river the water comes from. Try some—it will tear your guts out."

I was horrified to see Dooley put the cup to his lips and drink with only the slightest grimace. Then the old man refilled the bowl and passed it to me.

"Good heavens, Tom," I said, "this common cup is probably alive with germs and the old man himself has t.b.!" Tom growled. "Drink it, you damn fool, or at

82

least sip some of it! You can't insult this man's kindliness."

I took one swallow and nearly died, as much from the thought as from the vile taste. Then old Wong offered us a bowl of peanuts, and we each took a handful. I ate them to get the taste of the whisky out of my mouth. And they weren't bad—although not exactly roasted, they probably had been toasted in the sun.

As we walked along, Tom laughed and said, "Don't be squeamish, Paul. Everything's probably alive with germs up here, and a few strange bugs probably won't harm you. But you must always remember that these poor people are blessed with their own wonderful brand of pride and dignity. I wouldn't do anything to offend them or make them think that I'm another one of those superior white men."

I thought of this as I waited for Tom and Earl to return that morning. It was after five o'clock when they got back. Earl looked positively bushed, but Dooley looked fresh and untired except for the need of a shave.

I said, "That was old Wong, the Mekong whisky man, wasn't it?"

"Why, Paul! How did you know?" Tom seemed surprised that I had witnessed the incident, and pleased because I had recognized Wong's son. "Yes, it was poor old Wong. I guess he's not long for this world. We gave him a shot, and he's no longer hemorrhaging. But we had to stick around for a while, because it sure looked like curtains for poor old Wong this time."

Sleepy-eyed Earl offered me some coffee, but I yawned and said I thought I would go back to bed for a while. Tom just went back to his dictating machine and took up where he had left off.

I lay there in the next room, not wanting to sleep, but reminding myself that, whatever it was I had come to Laos looking for, I had found it—beyond any doubt. No one could ever make me doubt the sincerity of Tom Dooley, the physician and the man.

*March 30-31.* A few days after Paul Hellmuth's departure, Dooley told Dwight Davis: "Have Jerry Euster bring down your best suit and also Earl's. Tell him to have them pressed first and hang them in the plane so they won't get wrinkled. You will also need white shirts, ties, handkerchiefs—everything including shined shoes, no boondockers. And see to it that he has everything here before the 29th."

Dwight Davis says: "This was all very mysterious. We always kept our civilian clothes stored in the hotel in Vientiane, because we had no need for such fine apparel in Muong Sing. But this didn't make much sense, because we were scheduled to fly to Vientiane on March 30th for our departure from Laos next evening.

When Dwight pressed Dooley for further information, all he got was a broad grin and the cryptic remark: "Well, the King's coming to Muong Sing on March 30th, and we have got to put on a good show."

For the next week there was great activity in the village. The streets were cleaned, the houses decorated, and the old French fortress, now the base of the beefed-up Royal Lao garrison across from the Medico hospital, was draped with the national colors. This time a floral arch was erected at the little airstrip. The news was broadcast that the village school would be closed on the great day, and children and parents were instructed to turn out in their best finery.

Earl Rhine reports:

On the morning of March 30th we all bathed, shaved, and got dressed in our city clothes, with white shirts, neckties, shined shoes and even pocket handkerchiefs. Dooley lined us up and gave us a regular military inspection. This was going to be strictly a Class A occasion.

We got in the jeep and drove to the airport. The place was jammed and everything looked very festive. Then the Royal Lao Air Force plane arrived and his Majesty, King Savang Vathana stepped out followed by his entourage. He walked the three miles from the airport to the old fortress. The streets were lined with people bearing flowers and little bouquets which they tossed at the King. We all marched along behind him, and by that time we were really sweating in our city clothes under the mid-day sun. We followed the royal party into the fortress where the troops were lined up for the King's inspection. We were surprised when Tom Dooley led us to the place of honor beside the governor of the province. Then came the big surprise—Dwight and I were to be decorated. Both of us were completely flabbergasted, and we had no idea how we were supposed to act. Tom Dooley had not told us a thing.

Fortunately the governor was being decorated and, of course, he took precedence. We watched him carefully and decided to do exactly what he did. When the

King stepped up to him, the governor got down on his knees and made the usual Lao *sathoo*—hands before face with fingertips touching and the head slightly bowed. The King reached down and pinned the medal on him. Dwight was next in line, and as the King approached, Dwight started to kneel, but the King placed both hands on Dwight's shoulders and said: "Stand up, lad. There is no need for you to kneel."

Thus, Dwight and I received the Order of the Million Elephants and the White Parasol, the same beautiful decoration—a large and very ornate medal on a long red and gold ribbon—which Tom Dooley had received from the King a little more than a year before. The King, who is about fifty years old, has a remarkable voice and speaks perfect English. He told us that the people of Laos, and particularly those in Muong Sing, would be indebted to us forever for the kindness and generosity we had shown in taking care of their sick people. "You have brought to us the real heart of America and we shall never forget you." Dwight and I were really choked up.

Late that afternoon Earl Rhine and Dwight Davis, still dressed in their city clothes, said farewell to the many friends they had made during their 18 months in Muong Sing. Then they joined Tom Dooley and Jerry Euster and flew to Vientiane. On the evening of March 31 there was a big party in their honor, attended by many representatives of the Lao government and the American colony in Vientiane. At the airport Tom Dooley bade them goodbye. "When I was in Omaha last November I promised Emily and Esperanza that I would get you both home as near April Fool's day as possible so now it's time to get going. Goodbye, and God bless you. You are both fine men and your families will always be proud of what you have done."

# PART THREE

# 1960:

# SPRING

*April 7-10.* Of all the places he knew in Southeast Asia, next to Muong Sing, Tom Dooley loved most the city of Saigon, capital of the Republic of South Vietnam. In 1954-55, when he was struggling in the quagmires of Haiphong in the north, the southern city of Saigon was the distant and dubious haven of his 600,000 casualties on the "Passage to Freedom." Many of them, providentially, had made it. So, in the spring of 1960, whenever he flew in to Saigon he was always certain to be met by friends.

The former Commissioner of Refugees in Haiphong was now the Minister for Resettlement in the republic. The former mayor of Haiphong was also an important figure in the government, and the former president of the Hanoi Chamber of Commerce was now the owner of one of Saigon's large hotels. Saigon was full of priests, nuns, and former shoeshine boys whom he had rescued from under the descending Bamboo Curtain five years before. And there was always Madame Vu-Thi-Ngai, Director of the An-Lac Orphanage, and "Mother of a Thousand Children."

"When my spirits were unusually low," Tom Dooley once wrote, "I would get into my jeep after sundown and drive to the An-Lac Orphanage, where there was always laughter." Now in April 1960, when the old spirit was tired, and his mood often low, Tom Dooley came to Saigon on important business, knowing that he could count upon the gracious hospitality of Madame Ngai and a new generation of laughing kids to give surcease to his troubles.

Early in April he landed in Saigon late one evening and told the driver to take him to the An-Lac Orphanage, which was now located just a few blocks from the presidential palace. When they drew up to the padlocked gates of the high-walled enclosure, Tom Dooley got out and rapped for admittance. After much questioning and grumbling, the tall gate was opened by a small and wrinkled old lady who peered at him and then gave a shrill cry of recognition: *"Bac Sy My! Bac Sy My!"* She closed the gate and ran through the compound shrieking at the top of her voice that the *Bac Sy My* (American Doctor) had arrived.

Slowly sounds came from the corrugated steel buildings (Quonset huts), and then the compound rang with children's voices. Kids swarmed from the huts and engulfed the frail, tired, figure of the *Bac Sy My*. All at once he seemed to shed his troubles and his years.

With the children clutching his clothes and clinging to his legs, Tom Dooley happily pushed his way to the lighted doorway where he clasped his hands before his face and bowed his head in the traditional Asian greeting to Madame Vu-Thi-Ngai.

She looked exactly as he had seen her in the dark days of 1954—a small, beautifully proportioned woman with beautiful skin, jet-black hair and radiant dark eyes. "She must have been in her sixties," Tom had written in 1955, "but she could easily pass for a fashionable forty." Five years later, that casual compliment seemed to him like a gross understatement.

Madame Ngai, still the Tonkinese aristocrat, unchanged by the troubled years, led him into the "drawing room" of her Quonset hut mansion, where Dooley was not at all surprised to find a group of guests—a bishop, a priest, several government officials and some high brass of the Vietnamese Army and Air Force—gathered over the after-dinner coffee. Madame Ngai drew him into the light, and shook her head sadly. "Tom, *mon cher*, you are much too thin. And you are very tired. May I give you a brandy?"

Tom Dooley embraced her and kissed her cheeks. "Surely," he said, "there is a bit of bourbon in the house?"

Madame Ngai excused herself and went to search for Dr. Dooley's favorite drink; somewhere she was sure there was a partly filled bottle of this American whisky, probably left over from his last visit. Her mind was crowded with memories, some joyous and some sad.

I first met Dr. Tom in the fall of 1954 [she recalls], not long before the evacuation of Haiphong. Madame Querville, the wife of the French admiral, who was helping me in our overcrowded orphanage, told me that a young American Navy doctor had just arrived in North Vietnam and was doing amazing work for our unfortunate people. "You will like him," she told me. "He is just about your son's age, and he plays the piano beautifully. Besides, he is a very good doctor and he is most gentle with little children." My boy was stranded in Paris when the Communists devastated our home in the north and I had not seen him since 1946. But Madame Querville's words were most heartening to me because so many of our children needed medical care.

I remember the beautiful morning when he arrived and greeted me in very good French: *"Bon jour,* Madame. My name is Dr. Tom Dooley. No relation, however, to that Right Reverend Irishman, Monsignor Dooley. (He was referring to the Archbishop of Vietnam.) I have wanted to meet you for a long time, and now I have come to help you."

He was tall, handsome, with bright blue eyes and long dark eyelashes. But, oh, so young looking! However, my first impression of Dr. Dooley was not entirely favorable. He seemed nervous, restless, and he talked too rapidly and moved about too fast. But his manner changed completely when he visited the little ones in our nursery. Never had I seen a man more patient, loving, and compassionate with little children. Soon I learned that behind his brusque, arrogant manner there was the devotion of a great doctor and the ideals of a great humanitarian.

Madame Vu-Thi-Ngai had been a wealthy woman
with a beautiful home in Thanh Hoa when the town
was ravaged and her husband killed by the Communist
Viet Minh in 1946. She escaped with only her jewelry
and a few blocks of gold leaf; but as she fled southward with the hordes of refugees, she began gathering
up abandoned babies and stray children along the
way. By the time she arrived in Haiphong, more than
six years later, her jewelry was gone, but she had
acquired nearly a thousand orphans. Behind her
stretched a string of five temporary orphanages or
shelters, each abandoned as Madame Ngai and Company moved on southward, always a few days ahead
of the victorious Communists in the French Indo-
China War. She used the last of her precious gold leaf
to found the sixth An-Lac Orphanage in Haiphong,
where Tom Dooley met her in the dark days of 1954.

Dr. Tom became my devoted friend and protector,
and he was the great benefactor of the An-Lac Orphanage, and the children loved him. He stood by us until
the very end.

I remember when, about a fortnight before the evacuation of Haiphong, I received a letter from my mother
in Hanoi. She was very old and she had remained in the
north when everyone else fled. Now she begged me not
to go to Saigon with the other refugees, but to rejoin
her in Hanoi.

When I discussed the letter with Tom Dooley, he
told me emphatically: "Madame Ngai, you must not go
to Hanoi. Your mother is a very old woman and the Viet

95

Minh will not molest her. But if you go to Hanoi the Communists will surely take you. Besides, what will happen to the children?

I decided to send a very old and faithful family servant to Hanoi with a verbal message for my mother, telling her about the children, who now numbered over a thousand, and explaining why I could not come. This faithful old fellow returned with a letter which read: "If you do not come to me in Hanoi, I will consider you dead." But he also gave me a verbal message from my mother: "Tell my daughter that she must take her children and leave for Saigon immediately. Tell her she goes with my blessings and that I will always pray for her."

Thus, we did move south in April 1955, taking with us what equipment we could aboard the U.S.S. *General Brewster*. Tom Dooley, not only arranged everything, but he also communicated with the American Wives Club in Saigon and asked them to take care of us when we arrived.

These wonderful women took over and, thanks largely to their help, we now have our wonderful An-Lac Orphanage in Saigon.


Late that night, after the other guests had left, Tom Dooley sat talking to Madame Ngai, making light of his own troubles, and discussing at length his plans for a Medico hospital in South Vietnam.

"He told me that he had wanted to locate this new hospital up near the 17th parallel," says Madame Ngai. "But our president, Ngo Dinh Diem, who is a great admirer of Dr. Tom Dooley, wanted the hospital located at Quang Ngai, which is about two-thirds of the way up the coast. I did my best to convince Tom that the president's choice was the wise one. I had seen with my own eyes the horrible conditions in Quang Ngai, and I told him of the many mothers there who died in childbirth for want of medical care. As a matter of fact, I told him, many of the little ones in our nursery were brought to us from Quang Ngai."

The next morning Dooley walked over to the palace and accepted the president's proposal for a Medico hospital and a clinic at Quang Ngai. That same afternoon he took off in the Piper Apache to inspect the site, accompanied by the Deputy Minister of Health and Madame Vu-Thi-Ngai.

They flew east from Saigon, then northeast over the lush, green rice bowl of Vietnam until they sighted the South China Sea and the long coastline of white-sand beaches. Quang Ngai is a small coastal city that once was a popular seaside resort. Even now it can boast of such niceties as paved streets and Western-style houses with electric lights and running water, yet it is obviously a little city that has seen better days.

Six or seven years before, the government had started construction of a small hospital in Quang Ngai. But in 1954-55, when the city was repeatedly raided and pillaged by the Communist Viet Minh, the project was abandoned. Early in 1960, probably in anticipation of Tom Dooley's acceptance of the assignment, President Ngo Dinh Diem had ordered work resumed, and when Dooley arrived in Quang Ngai in April the hospital project was nearing completion. He reported to New York that "Quang Ngai is going to be a wonderful place."

The main building was a typical mud-and-straw structure with a thatched roof; the walls reached only about four feet above the ground with open space above to permit free circulation of air in the "wards" which Dooley estimated would accommodate 200 patients. There were also three "hard" (Western-style) buildings, the largest of which was to house the operating room and X-ray section. This had already been wired for electricity, but the cables ended at a rough concrete stand in the yard where the generator would be installed. The generator, like all other equipment for the empty buildings, would have to be furnished by Medico. The Vietnamese government would provide only the buildings, upkeep, gasoline, lights, transportation, etc., and pay the salaries of the Vietnamese personnel.

A young Vietnamese doctor, Sau Baa, had been assigned to the Quang Ngai hospital and was already living in one of the partially finished buildings. Actually, he was a *médecin indochinois*, with the equivalent of a high-school education plus training as a medical corpsman. But Dooley reported that Sau Baa was genuinely excited by the prospect of working with an American doctor and thus improving his medical training.

"Doctor Sau Baa thoroughly understands," said Dooley, "and Madame Ngai made very sure of this, that we are not going to rob him of his dignity or cause him to lose face with the local people. On the contrary, we want him to participate in everything to the degree that his ability and training will permit, and by working with an American physician and surgeon Dr. Baa's knowledge and skill will increase in time. He knows this."

Tom Dooley envisioned a future, only a few years distant, when South Vietnam would have its own graduate doctors to supplant the *médecins indochinois*, who were a hangover from the French colonial period. Already scores of Vietnamese boys and girls on scholarships were studying in American and European colleges and medical schools, and the time was not distant when they would be returning to repay the government for their education with so many years in the public health service.

"But what will happen if these ambitious well-educated young doctors return and there are no hospitals in which to serve?" Dooley asked. "Such a situation is unthinkable in a progressive country like this. The need now is not for a giant medical center, but small, modern, adequately equipped hospitals in the towns and districts where the young Vietnamese doctors can serve the people's needs. That is what we are providing in Quang Ngai, and it will be a model, the first of many."

On the plane, flying back to Saigon, Tom Dooley told Madame Ngai his immediate plans. He would go to Kuala Lumpur in Malaya to check on the status of the agreement Dr. Comanduras had recently negotiated for a Medico hospital in the adjacent town of Kuala Lipis. From there he would make plans for his return to the United States.

Tom Dooley's doctors had consented to his working in Asia only on the condition that he would return to New York for periodic checkups, and the first was due in early May. He was aware of the need for constant vigilance, and there may even have been some apprehension in his mind. Early in April he had written to Gloria Sassano, Medico Executive Secretary, suggesting dates for the fund-raising lectures he hoped to make while at home.

"But make arrangements with the Memorial doctors first," he added. "Tell them that, in addition to whatever else they plan to do. I want them to work up a complete series liver-function tests, no matter how long I have to remain in the hospital to get it done. They will know what I have in mind."

*April 21-24.* The long awaited *Life* article appeared in the April 18 issue, and Dooley saw a copy of it shortly before he left for the United States. But he had already heard about it in letters from shocked and indignant Medico supporters back home. Actually, it was neither sensational nor inaccurate but, as Paul Hellmuth has said, may have been marred by some misplaced emphasis.

Scot Leavitt's short article accompanying the picture pages stated: "The fact that Dr. Tom Dooley is a controversial figure in Southeast Asia astonishes most American visitors. The fact that he is not controversial in the U.S. astonishes their compatriots in Southeast Asia."

"Criticism of Dooley," said Leavitt, "falls into two main categories: 1) his personality irritates some people, and 2) his performance as a doctor seriously concerns others." The article strongly implied that Dooley merely put on a good show for the benefit of Americans who visited Muong Sing. Referring to "the Bear-mauled Man" (who appeared in one of the large photographs), Leavitt stated that the bear-mauled man was a hill tribesman who several years ago lost much of his face to a wounded bear. "Dooley likes to display him to visitors as a spectacular and horrible exhibit." Paul Hellmuth maintains that there was not one but several bear-mauling cases among Dooley's patients. Bob Copenhaver says: "That is absolutely correct. Such incidents are by no means uncommon in northern

101

Laos. When I was in Muong Sing in November 1960, I saw one fellow (and he was not the 'Bear-mauled man' pictured in *Life*) with a gaping and badly infected wound where his nose had been torn off. I remember the boys called him 'No-Nose Magoo.'"

What hurt Tom Dooley more than the article itself were the aggrieved and critical letters he received from people who had been his friends and supporters. There was one letter from a high school student in Massachusetts whose class had taken up a collection to support Dooley's work: "We sent you money to help you take care of the poor and sick people in Asia, and not to enable you to take pretty girls riding on the back of your fancy motor scooter."

Still, Scot Leavitt did try to strike a reasonable balance in his conclusion: "It is too bad that Dooley and his supporters have tried to depict him as a saint. He is not. It may be that only a man like Dooley, with an unyielding, belligerent faith in himself, could have accomplished what he has in Laos. And it may be that only a real saint could have done it without exasperating and angering so many people."

When reporters in Singapore and New York asked about his reaction to the article, Tom Dooley tried to dismiss it lightly and quoted what he said was an old Chinese proverb: "Man who raises head above bushes gets hit with rotten egg." But his intimate friends and family insist that he was deeply hurt.

His long-promised replacement in Muong Sing had not yet arrived, but in Bangkok Tom Dooley found an elderly doctor who agreed to serve as a substitute until he returned or until another doctor was sent to northern Laos. "Dr. Hautmann is a sixty-year-old man, Viennese by birth, who has done a lot of medical missionary-type work in Indonesia. He is an extremely gentle and simple man and I'm sure he will bury himself in the work. There is absolutely no question about his devotion. Actually, I would like to keep him with us permanently but I fear he is too old. The Ban Houei Sai hospital should be finished by the time he gets up there, and he can commute every couple of days from place to place, and keep things fairly well under control. However, he is not too enthusiastic about flying, and since he has a family living in Switzerland, I have promised that we will provide him with some kind of airplane accident insurance. Please ask Paul Hellmuth to see what can be done about this."

*May 1-8.* After holding brief conferences in Kuala Lumpur and Singapore, Tom Dooley boarded a jet in Bombay on May 1 and flew to Nairobi in Kenya, Africa on the first leg of his journey to the States. He spent two days with Dr. Mungai Njoroge, a native of Kenya who received his medical education at Stanford University School of Medicine and the Columbia University College of Physicians and Surgeons. Dr. Njoroge was in charge of the Chania Clinic, at that time the only African-operated hospital in all East Africa, located about thirty miles northeast of Nairobi. "Lack of medical facilities and trained personnel to treat Kenya's population of six million is one of that country's greatest problems," Dooley's report stated. "There are only four Africans in Kenya with M.D. degrees, Dr. Njoroge being one of them, and the only one at present who is carrying medicine beyond the cities."

Dooley now completed plans to support Njoroge's clinic and help him set up a Medico installation in Riruta, another village about 20 miles west of Nairobi. Dr. Njoroge reports:

Dr. Dooley now looked taller, thinner and a much sicker man than when I had last seen him six months earlier. His determination, however, had not changed. He was impatient to get his physical checkup and his business in New York over with because he felt he was wasting a lot of valuable time that should have been put into the opening of his new clinics in Southeast Asia.

To my mind he had no doubt whatsoever that he would be dead within a year. He did not show any fear, doubt or hesitancy about what had to be done during his remaining months. If anything, he intended to intensify his activities.

In Nairobi he was entertained at a number of parties, and when he talked of his work in the jungles and even of his own illness, he did so in a way that made guests envy him rather than pity him. To me alone, and privately, in the very last moments of his visit, he indicated that his visit probably would be the last he would ever make to Kenya, and he made no effort to disguise the seriousness of his condition.

At the same time, he gave me every assurance that he believed in what I was doing in Africa and that he would do everything possible in the remaining months to see that our Kenya clinics were given the fullest support. This gave me great assurance, and made me feel that Tom Dooley was the one human being closest to me ideologically, and that we shared common goals. I also committed myself and told him that the joint work that he and I were doing would continue in Africa so long as the spirit of our agreement remained. Tom Dooley was one of the best friends I have ever had."

From Nairobi he flew to Rome. During his three days there he had a private audience with Pope John XXIII, was entertained by the Notre Dame Club and gave a few talks before American groups in the Holy City. While in Rome he also received an unpublicized honor which remained unknown outside the Dooley family until after his death.

*May 8-12.* The checkup at Memorial Hospital took two days; then Tom Dooley reported to his new and quite presentable office in Medico's suite in the Graybar Building. He placed a call to Bob Copenhaver in Omaha and Bob was summoned to his second tour of active duty. Medico had lined up 55 speeches in 41 cities between May 15 and June 24.

Concerning his physical condition, as revealed by

the various tests, Dooley offered only the terse explanation: "So far, so good." Those closest to him were satisfied that the results had been negative. The X-ray examinations and the tests of his blood, lymph, tissues and liver function gave no indication of the cancer's spread. But Tom Dooley knew too well the nature of his disease to derive unwarranted confidence from such negative findings less than a year after his operation. He promised his doctors faithfully that he would return for a further checkup in October—five months hence. Meanwhile he intended to carry on, hopefully and with prayer.

Although he was never Tom's attending physician, Dr. Peter Comanduras, Secretary-General of Medico, was the one doctor who had been closely associated with Tom before and during the period of his grave illness. Together they had evolved the Medico concept at a meeting in Washington in November 1957. Dr. Comanduras, a distinguished Washington physician and an associate professor of Clinical Medicine of George Washington University Medical School, had agreed to give up his practice and his faculty post to become administrative head of the new organization.

"Dr. Comanduras has what I lack—the experience, temperament and ability to plan and direct operations," Tom Dooley wrote at that time. "I see myself as just another worker in the vineyard."

Says Peter Comanduras:

I had been with Tom in Southeast Asia earlier in
1960, so I was not as surprised as were other people
when he arrived in New York in May looking so thin
and exhausted. Work in Southeast Asia is always exhausting and particularly so to Westerners. Most people
who work in these primitive areas where the climate is
very hot and humid find it a very enervating experience.
So did Tom, but Tom Dooley never knew when to stop.
He actually drove himself from morning through the
night, day after day, and month after month without
ever taking a break. One could hardly keep up with
him, even after he had undergone this radical surgery.

However, after a few weeks in the United States, and
even during his lecture tours, he seemed to put on
weight and look much better. Even during the spring
of 1960, only nine or ten months after the operation, he
really gave people the impression that he was beating
the cancer statistics and that perhaps some miracle had
been performed. This was because he looked so well,
was always in high spirits, and kept driving himself at
his usual pace, while at the same time showing no out-
ward signs that the disease was actually slowly spreading through his body. Once or twice when we were
alone, we did talk about his chances of surviving the
malignant melanoma. He knew the facts and faced
them squarely. While no one could predict his fate, or
say whether he would survive six months or six years,
Tom knew that his future would be relatively brief in
any case.

But he made a truly remarkable effort to set aside
this consideration. I think this demonstrated one thing

—that Tom Dooley was a very practical person. He had work to do, things he was determined to accomplish, and he knew that if he permitted his mind to dwell upon his cancer he would get nowhere at all. Of course, there must have been terrible moments when he was all alone. But I don't think Tom really understood the words "worry" and "anxiety." If he did, he never allowed it to become part of his character, or to show up in his everyday activities and his everyday talk. Tom Dooley could put worry aside, and go on to the problem at hand, particularly the problem of Medico's progress.

This trait produced excellent results in all his activities. He concentrated on resolving problems, finding ways to get around difficulties, and when the solution did not come readily, he would set the problem aside and go on to the next one.

During 1959-60 I saw an entirely new and much greater Tom Dooley emerge. My first impression of Tom when I met him in Washington early in November 1957 was that of a young man devoted and dedicated to the proposition that he had something to offer to the world in his own way as an individual physician. It was apparent at that time that he did not quite appreciate the world-wide significance of what this represented. He had done a magnificent job in Laos entirely on his own. But he was obviously interested in the type of operation which he had at that time in Nam Tha, which was the forerunner of Muong Sing. This was a small out-patient clinic and a primitive hospital which one doctor could run with the help of two or three corpsmen or native nurses. He had not yet grasped the idea that once you begin giving modern American medicine to an emerging country in an under-developed area of the

108

world, it is important to give the best that American medicine can provide. Later on, as the Medico program developed, there was an obvious need to advance this type of village medicine by providing visiting specialists—surgeons, pediatricians, ophthalmologists, etc.—to back up the American general practitioners in charge, and to raise the local standards of medical education.

During the last year of his life, Tom Dooley showed a great capacity to adapt himself to this growing concept. When he visited Afghanistan, for example, and signed a contract with the Afghanistan government, he not only agreed to provide a complete Medico team to equip a 50-bed hospital, but he also suggested a provision for visiting specialists in surgery, internal medicine, etc., as well as laboratory and X-ray technicians. He made similar provisions in laying the groundwork for Medico teams in Malaya. He had come to realize that Medico must adjust itself to the situation in each particular country. For example, the village-type hospital, such as he had in Muong Sing, might be adequate at the moment for a country like Laos which has no medical school, no modern hospitals, no facilities like electricity or water supply which can maintain really modern medical service. But in more advanced countries, like Vietnam, Cambodia, Malaya, or Haiti, something better than the primitive village-type hospital must be provided.

So, despite his simplicity and his rather naïve attitude toward the practice of medicine in northern Laos, Tom Dooley came to realize that what was adequate for one country was insufficient elsewhere. Being a realist, above all else, Tom Dooley soon adjusted himself to a new situation.

*May 14-31.* Terrence Cotter, 27, a lean crew-cut graduate student at the University of Minnesota, was studying for a final exam in the Cotter apartment in Hastings, Minnesota, when the telephone rang.

"Terry Cotter? This is Dr. Tom Dooley in New York. I understand you and Jan would like to work with me in Southeast Asia. How about hopping on a plane and meeting me in Washington next week?"

Says Terry Cotter: "It took several seconds for the jolt to wear off, then I told him that my wife, Jan, was still at the hospital and that we would have to talk things over before I could make a definite date. Besides, I explained, I still had to take some finals for my Masters Degree in Political Science. Dr. Dooley told me to have a talk with Jan and call him back."

Jan Cotter, 27, a petite and very pretty girl who looks five years younger than her age, was then a graduate nurse in charge of a surgical ward of the Minnesota State Hospital in Hastings. On the evening of April 21, only a few weeks earlier, she and Terry Cotter had seen the one-hour documentary, *Biography of a Cancer,* on television. They decided that night that they would both like to serve for at least one year on a Medico team—Jan because she knew her professional services as a graduate nurse were sorely needed, and Terry because he felt that his four years of service with the Marines in Korea, London and Madrid should qualify him for the type of field work Dooley was doing. Besides, he said, he wanted to be

110

with Jan and the experience in Southeast Asia prob- ably would benefit his later career as a teacher of Political Science.

By mid-summer 1960, less than three months after Tom Dooley's telephone call, Jan and Terry Cotter were hard at work in the new Medico hospital at Ban Houei Sai. (They are still there, Jan as chief nurse, and Terry as the hospital administrator.)

Thus, in the spring of 1960, Medico's field personnel expanded. Where, originally, there had been one Dr. Tom Dooley, there soon were several Tom Dooleys— dedicated physicians and surgeons, some young and some in their middle years and one Negro woman doctor from the West Coast. These were supported by a score or more of nurses and corpsmen, like Jan and Terry Cotter, who were prepared to operate along the lines laid down by Dooley corpsmen from Norman Baker of the Haiphong refugee camps to Earl Rhine and Dwight Davis of Muong Sing.

The spring tour which took Tom Dooley and Bob Copenhaver from coast to coast and from Texas to Canada was devoted to more than speeches and fund raising. Tom Dooley had with him a file of carefully screened applications from aspiring doctors and corps- men, and in almost every large city he visited appli- cants were called in for personal interviews.

Bob Copenhaver tells the story:

I believe applications must have poured in to Medi- co's New York office by the thousands. There they were

111

screened by Dr. Comanduras and his staff, and by Tom Dooley when he happened to be in New York. The medical education and professional experience of the applying doctors were scrutinized carefully; equal care was devoted to the records of the graduate nurses. Screening the qualifications of the corpsmen, was more difficult, and prior to the personal interview, great weight had to be given to the service experience (Army, Navy, Air Force, etc.), and the motivation stated on the application blank.

Some of Dooley's reactions when he reviewed the screened applications were highly individualistic, to say the least. For example, the applicant is asked to state his reasons for wanting to join Medico and serve in the foreign field. I remember several people who stated their reasons with very lofty idealism, and one fellow in particular who said that he wanted to serve in Southeast Asia to "help uplift the depressed and impoverished yellow race."

"Get rid of that guy," Dooley would say. "We can't be bothered with psychos or crackpots."

Strangely, he was particularly hard on Catholics and others with pronounced religious training or convictions. He was determined that any form of religious proselytizing must never become a part of Medico's field operations.

I remember one man in particular, whose name I will omit for obvious reasons, who stated in his application that he had only recently left the seminary because, while he was a devout Catholic, he had found that he did not possess a true religious vocation. Tom gave him such a severe grilling that the fellow became almost white with anger; I was present and I wouldn't have

112

blamed the fellow if he had taken a poke at Tom. Dooley accused him of wanting to be a covert missionary and he implied strongly that he was going to Asia only to convert people. However, the boy reacted perfectly. He was accepted and became one of Medico's best men.

Dooley had another trick which he used to test an applicant's sincerity and resourcefulness. He would telephone at some off hour, preferably in the middle of the night, and tell the applicant to meet him in some distant city the next day. I remember arguing that this was unfair and unreasonable.

"Suppose he doesn't know how to get there," I said, "or suppose he doesn't have the money for plane fare?"

"If they want the job sincerely and bad enough they will get there. If they haven't got the money, let them borrow it. The point is that they must show sincerity and resourcefulness. Won't they need resourcefulness and even the ability to scrounge around when they're really up against it in some Asian mudhole?"

I remember once when Tom forced me to apply this technique to a promising young doctor in Oklahoma. Dr. Clint Chambers had just finished his internship in Oklahoma City, and his application indicated that he was a sound country boy, and just the sort of man Medico needed. He had worked at everything from a common laborer to an orderly in a mental institution in order to get through medical school.

While Tom stood by I called him up in Oklahoma City. The conversation went something like this:

"Dr. Chambers?"

"Yes, this is Clint Chambers."

"Clint, I am calling for Dr. Tom Dooley. He wants to

see you in New York. Get on a plane and meet us in the lobby of the Waldorf at five o'clock on Thursday afternoon."

"Shucks, I have never been to New York. How do you get there? Where is this hotel?"

"Take American Airlines—they fly all the way. The hotel is on the corner of Park Avenue and 50th Street. Be there."

Clint Chambers grumbled, very properly I thought, but he finally said okay. He met us in the Waldorf the next Thursday afternoon at 5:00 p.m. sharp. He turned out to be everything that Dooley had hoped for and he was immediately assigned to the new hospital that was being opened up at Ratanakiri, Cambodia.

When they met Tom Dooley for the first time, some of the M.D. applicants found it a rather bewildering experience. Being unfamiliar with Dooley's methods, and unaware that their backgrounds and experience had been thoroughly investigated, they considered some of his questions presumptuous or impertinent, or they were bowled over by what seemed to be his snap judgments:

"Okay, you leave next month. We'll meet in Hong Kong. You will go to work at —. Get a map and look it up."

Carl Wiedermann, 32, a tall, sensitive, mild-mannered man who looks like a young Abe Lincoln, was interviewed by Dooley while the latter was in Memorial Hospital undergoing the series of tests. Says Wiedermann:

114

He impressed me as being a very dynamic person, and I had read somewhere that he was a self-proclaimed extrovert. The room was full of people, and he was lying on the bed, dressed in a robe and blue pajamas. But he was constantly jumping up either to answer the telephone or greet someone or say goodbye.

We had very little opportunity to talk privately; he merely told me that I was to take charge of the new hospital at Quang Ngai, Vietnam. He said he was being discharged from the hospital in two days and was going down to Texas to make some speeches. I was completely flabbergasted when he asked: "Why don't you come to Texas with me?"

I dislike the idea of lecture tours and of being a social butterfly. But I knew now that I was going to Vietnam for Medico and I wanted to know more about my assignment. This seemed to be the only occasion I would have to discuss the plans with him. So we made arrangements to meet in Dallas.

I arrived in Dallas and received word that he would meet me in Lubbock. When I arrived in Lubbock and stepped out of the plane I received the shock of my life. They had rolled out a red carpet and several hundred people were waiting for the arrival of Dr. Tom Dooley. I felt terrible. I tried not to step on the red carpet and to make people know that I was certainly not Dr. Dooley. There was no need to do that; everyone knew what Dr. Dooley looked like. Nevertheless, they gave me the keys of the city and a few hours later Dooley's plane arrived.

I was with him in Texas for three days, and that was the first time I saw him in action. He was amazing—a real ball of fire. He had terrific stamina and he could

115

go from one speech to another. He could hold the audiences in the palms of his hands. And these audiences varied from college kids to Texas millionaires who paid twenty-five dollars a piece to hear him at dinner. But he always kept the audience in his hands. He was fantastic! And I can't say it was his way of speaking which impressed me so much. It was his whole personality.

Before leaving him and returning to New York alone, I asked him: "Tom, what is the truth about your health?"

He turned around and looked at me sharply. "Why do you ask me this? Do you ask me as a friend or as a doctor?"

"I am just asking you out of curiosity," I said. "I'm joining Medico, and am going to work with you and I want to know what the score is."

He thought for a moment and then said: "Carl, I think this thing is metastasizing to my lungs and probably to my bones. I'm pretty sure I haven't got more than eight or ten months to live." He said it with such simplicity that I was speechless.

I asked him then: "What keeps you running around giving speeches, going back to Asia? If it were me, I would relax and take life easy. I would go to the Isle of Capri, where I lived years ago, and would spend my remaining days savoring the good things of life."

At first he didn't answer. Then he asked me about a certain dancer and about a number of people in the international set on Capri. Did I know them? Then he spoke quite familiarly about people who travel in this fast crowd, a group you can only meet in places like Capri. I looked at him with surprise. He was a completely new person.

116

The first thing I did when I got back to New York was to take back many of the things I had said before I really got to know Tom Dooley. I tried to make it clear to everyone that I considered him quite a guy.

Not everyone was captivated by the Dooley personality, however. Dr. Ronald M. Wintrob, 25, says he "had a very intense dislike of Tom from the first time I met him, and subsequently an even greater dislike. I bitterly resented his arrogance, lack of consideration, ignorance of common courtesy."

Ronald Wintrob had been hired by Dr. Peter Comanduras for a one-year tour of duty in Southeast Asia. "I was extremely busy at that time on the obstetrics service of Kings County Hospital in New York. With great difficulty I was able to get to Medico's office for a 9:00 A.M. appointment with Tom. At 11:30 A.M. he talked with me for a few minutes; then he asked me to walk to the Waldorf with him. By one o'clock he had not said more than ten sentences bearing directly on my activities with Medico, except that he would find something for me to do."

Strangely, it was Dr. Ronald Wintrob who was chosen to take over Dooley's favorite post—Muong Sing.


*May 3.* The measure of Tom Dooley's accomplishments in the first half of 1960 appears in a report he made at the annual dinner of the Medical Society of the State of New York in May. From two small hospitals and a mere handful of men, Medico's field operations had been expanded to eleven projects in seven countries staffed by twelve doctors and more than thirty American nurses and corpsmen. He summed up:

> We have a Cambodian Hospital, run by Dr. Manny Voulgaropoulos, and we have a new hospital being built in Cambodia in the town of Ratanakiri. We have a new hospital that is being built by the Vietnamese government and we provide medical services for the largest orphanage in Saigon.
>
> In Laos we have just built a new village hospital in a town called Ban Houei Sai, and, as perhaps you know, Dooley has a small hospital in a town that quivers on the frontier of Red China, a town called Muong Sing.
>
> In Malaya we have just signed an accord with the Malayan government to dispatch a team to Kuala Lumpur next month.
>
> In Kenya, we have a young Kikuyu doctor, Dr. Mungai Njoroge, who is doing an excellent job, and we have just pledged him a $25,000 new clinic which will go into construction immediately.
>
> One of our largest projects is a medical service in Haiti, where we work with Johns Hopkins University and the Henry Ford Hospital. We have teams or support programs in Gabon, in Peru, in Jordan, in Afghanistan, and other projects around the world.
>
> These are not plans and programs in the blueprint stage; these are *existing* programs. They are there now in operation and those that do not have full staffs will have them very soon.

These are simple programs. The global planners are indubitably scoffing at us and I couldn't care less. These programs each have satellite activities around them—the simple village hospital has a half dozen clinics in the mountains around it. But each team is an intimate part of the village life; each team doctor goes to the weddings and to the funerals. Each team doctor is a part of that community life. We don't come in, spend a few weeks and then pull out—we are part of the community. And because this idea has become beloved in Asia, the host governments put up what we need. The host governments pay all indigenous salaries; the host governments build the buildings and give us warehousing and internal transportation and carte blanche for the medicines the host governments possess.

One question is always asked of those who go out in the world and leave behind them certain accoutrements of civilization, and that question is "Okay, buddy, what do you get out of it?" Well, ladies and gentlemen, I can speak for all of these young doctors—because I've been in this business of village medicine for six years—and I'll tell you what I get out of it. I get plenty.

All of us have the same quiet, inner joy that you have when you see your patients' eyes light up just a little bit because of you. But take that patient and put him in a hospital, in a high mountain valley, half a world away, where without you he has black magic or sorcery; you heal him and the glow inside you is a thing that is full of wonder. We who are in this field have formed a new purpose and a new order in our lives. And we have a fulfillment of man's normal appetite for fruitful activity and a high purpose in life.

We have the satisfaction of doing a job that needs

119

doing—not by a government but by individual Americans. We have that feeling of accomplishment. We feel good in our hearts when we know that we are giving meaning to the fundamental yearning of all men in all lands everywhere, in our case by utilizing this wonderful weapon of medicine blended with compassion.

But our deepest reward is knowing that we of Medico in some small way are helping to fulfill a dream—a dream that a young German Jewish girl wrote of in the furor of World War II—the dream of Anne Frank: "Things will change, and men become good again, and these pitiless days will come to an end, and the world will know once again order, trust, and peace."

*June 6.* Dooley went to South Bend, Indiana, to receive from his alma mater, Notre Dame, an honorary degree in the company of such distinguished recipients as President Dwight D. Eisenhower, and Cardinal Montini, Archbishop of Milan. At the luncheon for honored guests preceding the ceremonies, President Eisenhower asked Father Hesburgh, President of Notre Dame: "Where's Doctor Tom Dooley? I want to meet him and have a talk."

Dooley was seated beside the President and spent most of the time during luncheon answering Ike's questions about Medico's field operations, finances, logistics problems, and relations with foreign governments. At one point, Tom beckoned to his brother, Malcolm, who was seated at another table with his wife, Gay, and Malcolm went up to the head table.

"Mr. President, this is my brother Malcolm Dooley," said Tom. "He handles Medico's business affairs." There was an amusing aftermath to this perfunctory meeting, which Malcolm Dooley relates:

Later, we went outside and took our place in the audience seated on the campus. The academic procession took place and I saw Tom on the platform a few places away from President Eisenhower. Then a slip of paper was passed to me and I saw it was a message from Tom. His handwriting was never very legible at best, and this apparently had been written while he moved along in the procession. The note read: "You fly Ike. SS will contact."

This didn't mean a thing to me and I looked toward Tom and saw him making a lot of crazy gestures. He pointed toward the President, then to me, and then skyward. Then he flapped his hands like a bird flying. I began to get the idea, although it seemed highly improbable.

The campus, of course, was alive with Secret Service men, but now I noticed Jim Rowley, head of the White House detail, walking up the aisle and scrutinizing the audience with a worried frown on his face. He stopped and spoke to Father Wilson, who had been one of my instructors during my senior year at Notre Dame, and who was now acting as Notre Dame's liaison with the Secret Service. Father Wilson laughed and pointed at me and Jim Rowley beckoned for me to come with him.

"You are flying to West Point with the President," Jim Rowley said. Then, for the first time, I learned what it was all about.

While in the locker room, donning their academic

gowns, Tom had said to the President: "By the way, Mr. President, my brother is a busy man, and he ought to get back to New York. Couldn't you give him a ride on the Columbine?" President Eisenhower explained that he had interrupted his own 35th reunion at West Point to come out to South Bend, and he was returning there immediately. The President turned to his personal physician, General Snyder, and said: "Doc, have someone find young Dooley and make sure he gets in the motorcade. We've got to get right out of here as soon as the commencement is over."

At any rate, the next thing I knew I was surrounded by Secret Service men who pushed me through the crowd and into a four-door convertible Oldsmobile. The motorcade took off and I was speeding toward the airport, leaving behind my wife, my mother, Paul Hellmuth and Tom.

We had a wonderful flight eastward and finally landed at the Air Force base near West Point. There I said goodbye to the President and thanked him for the ride. I could see now that the Secret Service men didn't know what to do with me.

"Where are you going?" one of them asked.

"The Waldorf."

They went into a huddle, and then two of them put me in a Chevrolet and drove off at 75 miles per hour down the west side of the Hudson and over the George Washington Bridge. We arrived at the Waldorf about 9:00 P.M. I had no luggage, not even a shaving kit, but fortunately the night manager knew me and I was checked in without difficulty.

Before I went to bed that night, I wondered: What had been the big idea? Had this been another one of

Tom's gags? Or was he trying to impress me by getting me a through ride with the President aboard the Columbine?

Probably the big idea had in it a bit of both motives. Impulsive—and prankish—Tom Dooley had decided on the spur of the moment that it would be a big surprise for his brother to find himself flying east in the President's company, and it would give Malcolm something with which to impress his five small children. Tom's hunch was correct on both counts. Many days later the Malcolm Dooleys were surprised to overhear little Maureen telling her playmates: "My daddy went flying halfway around the world with the President, General George Washington."

*June 19.* Many people have remarked that during this period Tom Dooley seemed to be reaching out for old friends. Bob Copenhaver and Tom's brother, Malcolm Dooley, noticed that he would often schedule dates or even change lecture engagements in order to be in a certain city at a time when he could be with people who were part of a cherished past.

Such an occasion, apparently, was the wedding of Bart Hogan, an old Navy friend and the son of Rear Admiral Bartholomew W. Hogan ("The Skipper"), who had been the Navy's Surgeon General when young Tom Dooley attained fame on the "Passage to

Freedom" operation out of Haiphong in 1955. At the Hogan wedding Dooley saw many old and dear friends, but none he loved and respected more than Clare Murphy.

Clare Murphy, longtime secretary to the Surgeon General, is a slight, vibrant woman with light brown hair and sparkling blue eyes. With her sharp Irish wit and tart tongue she was a perfect match for Tom Dooley, and when they met for the first time in the Surgeon General's office early in 1956, they formed a lasting friendship marked by deep mutual respect.

Clare Murphy writes her recollections:

He was the snappiest, best-looking young naval officer I had seen in a long time, and he was blessed with a keen sense of humor and all the charm of his Irish ancestry. He always knew exactly what he was doing and where he was going, which made it a pleasure to work with him. Even at twenty-eight, he was master of the spoken and written word, and his dictation was perfect and so fascinating you were sorry when he stopped. When it was transcribed, never a word needed to be changed. He was a secretary's dream from that angle alone.

He was always in a hurry, and the consensus in the Navy Department was that if Dooley kept up the pace he was headed for a breakdown, either mental or physical. Neither ever happened to him, although the pace gained momentum in subsequent years.

After he returned from the Far East, he was attached to the Office of the Surgeon General for the first three months of 1956, and he worked out of my office.

During that time he made hundreds of talks at various naval activities, and at many colleges and universities. The public relations officers were wild about him, because he was in great demand and always made good copy. They could not get enough of him, and they regretted his decision to resign from the Navy in order to work in Laos, which he had to do as a civilian.

During his first year in Laos (1956-57), and until Medico was organized, I took care of his personal mail and whatever else needed to be done in the States. He offered to pay me a salary, but I refused because I had a responsible job of my own and could only give him what spare time I had. Thus, I was free to do as much or as little as I pleased, but the work intrigued me so that I never knew when to stop.

At that time, many people, and groups of people, were doing their best to put obstacles in Tom Dooley's way. I was determined to do everything I could to keep his valiant spirit from being trampled upon. And valiant was the word for Tom. He was remarkable when it came to rising above anything that seemed like an insurmountable obstacle. He handled that whole gigantic project [the Haiphong refugee camps] single handed; I can't think of any fifteen men who, collectively, could have accomplished it, or even would have tried with all the obstacles that were tossed in.

I thought that once he got to Laos on his own his troubles would be over. But the Americans there were anything but kind to him. However, they all lived to see the day when Tom Dooley was acclaimed as one of the ten outstanding men of the world.

While in the Navy, and under orders, he was easy to handle; but the minute he got out of the Navy and was on

his own he was like quicksilver. He always had so much
to do, and there never were enough hours in the day
or night in which to do it. He had no respect whatever
for the inventor of sleep, which even then he considered
a waste of valuable time when he had so much to accomplish. I am sure he never went to sleep until he
couldn't stand up.

I have seen him forget to eat breakfast and lunch,
and when he got lightheaded around four in the afternoon it suddenly dawned on him he had not eaten since
the day before. While he seemed to use good judgment
about everything else, he refused to admit that regular
meals and at least six hours sleep out of every twenty-
four might contribute to a longer life and certainly a
more comfortable one. The suggestion would make him
furious! I vowed he could drop dead before I ever
would mention it to him again. But then he would drive
himself so relentlessly that, against my better judgment,
I would find myself asking him just how long he thought
he could keep it up.

Occasionally he would write to me from Laos about
not feeling too well. One instance I recall with amusement. He wrote that his liver was "kicking up badly,"
and he thought he would have to get some doctor to
check it. I wrote back urging him to do so immediately,
and I reminded him that he only had *one* liver to give
to his own or anyone else's country.

He wrote a scorching letter in reply. How many
livers did I think he had—*three*? I replied in the same
tone: "I thought you *must* have a couple of spares,
because otherwise no one, and particularly a doctor,
would ever abuse the only *one* he had like you do."

126

After that he often signed his letters "Tom (Three-Livered) Dooley."

The odd part of it is that while he should have looked as time-worn as Dr. Schweitzer (who is old enough to be his great-grandfather), Tom Dooley went to his grave looking as though he was still eighteen.

Of course, there were many people who did not like Tom Dooley. But they usually were small people even though they were in high places. However, few of them ever dared to criticize him unjustly in my presence. Tom said many times that I was his "greatest champion and severest critic." I know he respected my judgment, and he was well aware of the fact that I did not think he was perfect. He knew he wasn't perfect, and he got weary at times of the people who tried to say that he was.

In July 1959 he wrote me that some French author had written a book in which he compared Tom Dooley to St. Augustine ("Just call me Gus!" he added). He offered to send me a copy. I wrote that I certainly would like to see *that* book with my own eyes, because no one but a Frenchman could think that one up! "If you're a saint, by any name, you sure wear your halo at a mighty crooked angle."

I was in Washington in August 1959 when Tom's trouble was diagnosed as cancer. He called me on the phone from New York. If Tom had hit me over the head with a club he couldn't have stunned me more. He admitted that he was "kind of shook up, too." On the morning of his first operation he telephoned me and said he was scared. I knew Tom Dooley didn't scare easily. I tried to kid him out of it by saying that I didn't think St. Peter would call him because I was sure Peter had enough problems without adding Dooley to his woes. He laughed and made me promise to come to see him that weekend. Surgery was performed on a Thursday, and on Saturday (August 27) I found him sitting up in bed, and on Sunday, when I left, he walked to the elevator with me. He said to the girl at the desk, "Nurse, I'm checking out!" She looked startled, and then, when she saw the bathrobe and pajamas, she laughed. Sick or well, Tom Dooley was never dull!

He wrote me a letter in Bangkok dated January 1, 1960: "Am definitely slowed up. Maybe it's being thrust into Asia's blistering heat again. Maybe it's just the long (or short) road downhill that I might as well prepare myself for." It turned out to be the short one.

During the spring of 1960, I saw Tom when he visited my home town, Worcester, Massachusetts, on his lecture tour, and then we met at Bart Hogan's wedding on June 19. Agnes Dooley, Tom's mother had become a dear friend of mine, and with her I was to see him again several times, some months later, but on much less happy occasions. I want to remember him as he appeared on that June day in Washington and on earlier days when he was the young, gay, dauntless Tom Dooley, a man with the spark of divine inspiration in his eyes and a sense of humor that would never let him be solemn about his destiny.

Tom was a deeply religious man; but how deep his faith was I didn't realize until much later. For one thing, he was never stuffy about it, never holier-than-thou like so many religious people I have known. He once wrote me that if he got to Heaven ahead of me he would see to it that the Golden Gates were all shined up in my honor, and that he would be there to reach out and pull me in. I told him he would have to pull hard, because I didn't think Heaven would be my first stop, largely because of my association with him while on this planet earth!

*June 20-30.* The spring lecture tour, combined with the interviewing of Medico volunteers kept Dooley and Copenhaver on the go through the month of June. Now Tom faced still another problem. Jerry Euster's six months as pilot of the Piper Apache had expired a month ago and Jerry was eager to get back to the States. A replacement had to be found immediately for by now Tom Dooley knew he could never get his job done without the airplane. Then he thought of Ted Werner, a young Navy fighter pilot who had been his good friend back in the pre-Indochina days when they were both stationed at Camp Pendleton in California and later at the Yokosuka naval base in Japan.

Ted Werner, seven years younger than Dooley, has been described as a Steve Canyon or "Terry and the Pirates" character—a tall, blondish, outdoors type who takes his flying seriously but aspires to a civilian career as a dental surgeon. He had only recently left the Navy in June 1960 when Tom telephoned him at the Werner family home in Los Angeles and offered him the job as Dooley's pilot.

"I was vaguely interested," says Ted Werner, "but I was also hesitant because I had already applied for admission to dental school and I had been accepted.

129

But I also knew Tom Dooley. Within a few days I had a wire from him: WILL ARRIVE LOS ANGELES SHORTLY. EXPECT YOU TO LEAVE FOR LAOS BEFORE JULY FIRST. PLANE TICKETS BEING MAILED. I knew then that Dooley had me hooked."

Ted Werner never regretted the move, although it set him back almost a year in his dental education and took him through some harrowing experiences. More than anyone else he was destined to eye-witness the decline and collapse of Tom Dooley during Tom's final days in Southeast Asia.

# PART FOUR

## 1960:

## SUMMER

*July 6-19*. In Los Angeles Tom Dooley met three more key members of his team—Dr. Estelle Hughes, 36, a Negro physician, Dr. Arlan Rosenbloom, 26, and his wife, Edith, who is a graduate medical technologist.

Dooley had been tremendously impressed by Estelle Hughes' record and the opinions of Dr. Comanduras and others who had interviewed her. Since graduating from Howard University School of Medicine in 1959, she had studied Spanish and Chinese. On her application blank she had stated: "I first heard of Medico when Dr. Comanduras spoke at Howard. What he said sounded to me like an answer to a prayer. My awareness of the need for doctors in some of the under-developed areas of the world dated back to my high-school days; and all through college and medical school my ambition to become a doctor of medicine was closely coupled with a hope that I might be able, somehow, to minister as a physician to sick people in some less privileged country where medical care of any kind is virtually nonexistent. Medico's

133

program of simultaneously taking care of patients and training native personnel seemed to me to be exactly what these countries need—medical know-how plus independence."

Both the Rosenblooms and Estelle Hughes were to serve in Cambodia, the Rosenblooms at Kratie and Dr. Hughes at the new hospital in Ratanakiri. But Estelle Hughes, a divorcee, has a 12-year-old son, Everard. Because conditions at Ratanakiri were primitive, and the hospital still under construction, Dooley later had Dr. Hughes transferred to Ban Houei Sai in Laos, where Everard Hughes was able to be with his mother.

"This was a wonderful thing for Doctor Tom to do and I think it is so typical of his deep understanding of people and of his warm heart," says Dr. Hughes. "The experience was an invaluable one for my son. He continued his school by a correspondence course, but he also attended the local school at Ban Houei Sai with the Lao children, which was also a broadening experience.

"Everard adored Dr. Dooley, and I think Dr. Dooley still holds a special place in Everard's heart. He always made Everard feel like he was a big and important person, as Dr. Dooley always did with people. He gave him such jobs at Ban Houei Sai as taking care of the paint brushes, making sure they were always cleaned with turpentine and carefully stored. Everard took this as a grave responsibility. Doctor Tom also gave him gifts, like the Scout pocket knife with many blades, and Everard still wears it on his belt."

When she was with Tom Dooley in California at that time, Dr. Hughes found it difficult to believe that this was the sick man who, according to most accounts, was dying of an incurable form of cancer.

"He seemed so vigorous and active, and he had the kind of infectious enthusiasm that made everyone associated with him want to work as hard and devotedly as he did. Of course, I didn't know him well at that time. Later, I began to see that he was putting up a brave front and concealing his true condition. He was driving himself relentlessly, and inspiring rather than depressing his co-workers was part of the job. But then the days came when he could no longer feign good health, and when those remarkable stores of energy were exhausted. Those are the days which I never shall forget."

*July 18-19.* Dr. Dooley was definitely in the mood for communing with old friends, and during his two-day stay in Hawaii he enjoyed a long visit with Jefferson Davis Cheek. Jeff was accompanied by his wife, Denise, and their 18 month old son, Dennis.

Dooley was delighted by Dennis who was then in the active walking-talking stage of development. But Jeff recalls that, at one point, as he sat watching the child, Tom grew very quiet. A strange sadness came into his face, and he said: "You know, Jeff, the great Tom Dooley envies you to beat hell right now."

"Then the mood passed," Jeff says, "and the mask was back in place. That was the only time I ever saw Dooley display anything resembling self-pity."

Jeff was one man Tom Dooley never could fool, and and Tom's bluff manner and apparent good health were transparent to the veteran newspaperman and government information officer who had known Tom Dooley since Dooley's first days as an independent operator in Laos. It was Jeff Cheek (always "Jeff Cheek of Comanche, Texas," in Dooley's books) who brought to Dooley's first hospital in Laos the little 14-year-old girl, Savong, whom Jeff had found lying abandoned and near death on a jungle trail. Dooley and his corpsmen worked a surgical and nursing miracle on the waif and restored her to complete health. (Tom told the story in *The Edge of Tomorrow*.)

Jeff Cheek writes from Honolulu:

On October 13, 1956, I arrived in Vientiane, Laos, where I was to be attached to the U.S. Information Agency for the next two years. At that time I had never heard of Dooley or of his work. He had already set up his first hospital in the small village of Vang Vieng some 175 miles north of Vientiane. But I heard plenty about Tom Dooley in the first few days after my arrival.

Dooley was very unpopular among the Americans of Vientiane. They were critical of his ego, his fanatical zeal, his flair for personal publicity. The more I heard, the more I wanted to meet the guy. So, on Thanksgiving

Day, 1956, I had my cook get up very early and start roasting a turkey. I figured that any American would appreciate a turkey on Thanksgiving, and I was pretty sure Dooley and his American team-mates didn't have one in Vang Vieng. By 7:00 A.M. the turkey was ready. I loaded my jeep with extra gasoline, extra food and Dooley's mail, which I had picked up. Then shoved off for Vang Vieng. I arrived there about eight hours later and just introduced myself as Jeff Cheek of Comanche, Texas, and the name stuck. The boys were bowled over by my American-style turkey dinner. And since the jungles of Laos abound with wild chicken, I had managed to bag a couple of wild chickens on my drive up to Vang Vieng. We all lived off chicken and dumplings for the next few days, instead of C ration, which was the usual fare for Dooley and his medics.

The house which Dooley and his team had chosen for themselves was no better or no worse than that of the other villagers. It was a three-room hut, made of bamboo, with the joints of the house secured by a vine called *wy* in the Lao language. But it had one item which differentiated it from all the others—a large American flag hung from a bamboo flagstaff on the front porch. The single concrete building which the villagers had offered Dooley had been rejected. It would serve to set the Dooley crew apart from the villagers they had come to serve. Instead, he converted that house into a hospital.

I got a fire going, and when Dooley and his boys came back from work, we all sat down to Thanksgiving dinner. To say that they came back from work is inaccurate, however. Actually they were always working. They got up in the morning to find patients waiting for them on the doorstep. While they ate breakfast or lunch or dinner, other patients materialized out of the jungle, and squatted patiently in the dust, waiting.

My first impressions of Dooley were these: He was a young man with tremendous driving energy, with a desire to get things done. He had an ego that was mountainous. He had absolutely no patience with mediocrity. He was brilliant in the intellectual sense, and full of charm which he could turn off and on as with a spigot.

I could see that these were the characteristics that people disliked in Dooley. But I soon learned that most people did not make the effort, as I and a few others did, to look behind the Dooley façade. There they would have seen a remarkable human being—a man full of deep love and pity for the suffering people of the world. They also would have learned two other things about Dooley.

First, that he was an extremely lonely person. This sounds fantastic, but it was true. He filled his life with good work, but he never found friendship. I guess Dooley never had more than a dozen close friends during his whole life. Out of this loneliness came the overpowering drive to make the world better, so that people would like (and perhaps love) him. My driving eight hours to bring him a turkey dinner touched him deeply. It was a simple act, given in friendship, by a total stranger. This touched him deeply, and he referred to it often in later years. To Dooley, it meant that *somebody* liked him. He was fighting a battle to win friends, and this was a victory.

Secondly, they would have learned that Dooley, while he was an excellent speaker and a gifted writer, really

suffered from a lack of communication. He could talk
at great length about projects that he was interested in.
He could sway people with his oratory, but he could not
communicate his inner feelings to anyone. I once told
him that, for this very reason, he would make some
woman the world's worst husband.

In those early days he could not speak a word of Lao.
So, when I visited him, I would go with him on sick call
to distant villages, serving as both driver and interpreter. We would stop in some little village. Dooley
would drop the tail gate of the jeep, set up his medicines, and treat anyone who came. I watched him
closely at these occasions. His manner became completely different. The inner tension disappeared, his
voice would soften, he would almost croon to the sick
children, as he gave them shots of penicillin, and
quieted them with a stick of candy or a toy balloon.
Here Dooley could let his guard down. He no longer
had to impress people. The need for communication
was gone. People loved him for what he was. Here
Dooley was safe.

That's when I saw the real Dooley emerge—a shy,
lonely man, ridden by doubts and fears, possessed with
a burning desire to help, but fearful that he would be
(and he was) misunderstood. And over all this I could
see his aching desire to communicate, to let someone
else know how he felt. But for some reason, known
only to himself, and perhaps his immediate family,
Dooley had built a wall around his heart, and this wall
was too high for anyone to ever see over it.

Dooley said many times that he was happy only when
working in Laos. Some Americans have ridiculed this
as a publicity gimmick, much as they used to hoot at

the late Carole Lombard for saying that she liked to pay taxes. They were wrong—Dooley *was* happy in Laos, if only because he could be himself out in the jungles where he did not have to mask his innermost feelings.

Dooley was a very practical person. On my first visit to his hospital at Vang Vieng, I did most of the cooking, simply because this freed him and his three medics for more important work. This task I volunteered for. But, later, Dooley said to me: "I have to make several night calls. I will wake you up and you can drive me." It never occurred to Dooley to *ask!* To him, this was the practical way to arrange things: The medics were busy all day, and *they* needed sleep. I could drive him, and interpret for him, as well as cook for him. I didn't resent this, but I remember that it did seem tactless, almost rude, at the time.

I remember one patient we handled on such a night call. He was a Lao male, about 40 or 45 years of age. He had come down with pneumonia. After the witch-doctors tried to cure him and failed, the family sent for the *"Khun Ma Farang"* (Friend Foreign Doctor). The messenger woke us at 3:00 A.M. A few minutes later we left for the village. Luckily the sick man lived in a village that could be reached easily by jeep.

The patient was near death when we arrived. Doc decided that he was too sick to move. He put the patient on an improvised stretcher, and elevated the lower portion of the body at a 30 or 35 degree angle. He constructed a crude vaporizer by using a *tao* (fire pot), an old blanket, and a length of bamboo attached to a tea kettle. This was nineteenth century medicine all right, but it saved that man's life. We returned at about 6:30 A.M. I stayed up to fix breakfast. Doc took a half-hour rest, then went right ahead with the day's work.

I needn't repeat here the well-known story of Savong, the little Lao girl that I brought to Dooley, and whose life he saved. But after Savong recovered, Dooley took a picture of her which he gave me on his next trip to Vientiane. Ever since, I have carried that picture in my wallet. Whenever I heard some loudmouth in Vientiane or Hong Kong sounding off about Dooley's ego and his phoniness, I would whip out that picture and say: "Dooley saved the life of this little girl. Tell me, how many lives have *you* saved?"

I left Laos in September 1958, and my wife and I settled in Hawaii. In August 1959, when I heard that Doc had cancer, I was stunned. I remember saying to my wife, Denise: "There are thousands of jerks in the world whom we could live without. Why does someone like Tom Dooley have to get cancer?"

When I saw Tom Dooley, an obviously sick man, in Hawaii in July 1960, I kept thinking: "There are lots of Savongs in northern Laos who owe their lives to you —babies, small children, pregnant women, old folks, people who would have died long ago in that land of filth, misery, poverty, and without doctors. There are lots of loudmouth Americans who also know this in their hearts. But there's something else that's more important. And that is that there are *people* in Vang Vieng and Nam Tha and Muong Sing who know that they are a little better off because you, Tom Dooley, the *Thanh Mo America*, happened to pass this way."

Before they parted that day in July 1960, Jeff asked Dooley to be the godfather of the baby the Cheeks were expecting in February. Tom was hesitant. "You must know," he said, "that my chances for survival are pretty slim. The Church might not accept me as a godfather." Jeff assured him that he had already made inquiries and that Dooley was acceptable. "All right," Dooley said. "Keep me posted through the embassy in Vientiane. If I'm still around in February, I'll be happy to lend my good name to your newest offspring."

Jeff Cheek writes: "When our son, David Jefferson Cheek, was born 17 February 1961, Doc had been dead for several weeks."

*July 20-22.* From Honolulu Tom Dooley had cabled Seiichi Fukuoka, editor of the Japanese edition of the *Reader's Digest,* saying that he would be in Tokyo on July 20-22 and would appreciate the opportunity to address any available groups of young doctors, medical students and social workers. This request at such a time, and on short notice, presented problems. Seiichi Fukuoka reports from Tokyo:

> This was the summer vacation period and there were few students in the universities, but I did find one large class of young social and medical workers who were attending summer school under the auspices of the National Social Welfare Association which seemed to meet his requirements perfectly. I also arranged for him to meet representatives of the Japanese and foreign press at the Foreign Correspondents Club on the morning of his arrival.
>
> But this was in the midst of the sweltering "dog days"

of the Tokyo summer and I worried about how Tom
Dooley would bear up under the weather and the
exertion of traveling in his present physical condition.
I had met him many times before during 1956-59 when
translations of his books appeared in the Japanese edition of the *Digest,* and I greatly admired him and considered him my friend.

When I first met him in 1956 I considered him the
typical social crusader, and his air of inspired self-
assurance reminded me somewhat of the late Dr. Toyohiko Kagawa, whose unlimited faith in himself seemed
to make him think that everyone should unconditionally
bow before him. But now, in July 1960, as I waited for
Dr. Dooley to arrive at the Tokyo airport, I was appre-
hensive and deeply troubled. When I was in Pleasant-
ville, New York, in March I had been told by the American editors that Dooley's cancer was of a malignant
type and that he did not have long to live. I had the
strange feeling of one waiting to greet a dying man.

But what I saw was nothing of the kind. Dooley came
off the plane and stood before me as cheerful and as
full of pep as ever, although somewhat thinner. There
was no suggestion of impending tragedy about him.
And nothing occurred to change this impression during
the three days we were together. There was, however,
one striking difference that I noticed almost immediately. The self-confident and perhaps slightly overbearing manner which, four years earlier, had made me
think of Toyohiko Kagawa seemed to have changed.
The Dooley I met in July 1960 was a different man.
There was now a greater warmth, even a certain humil-
ity, which gave one the first impression of a real
humanitarian.

143

After a few hours of sleep, Dooley appeared at the Foreign Correspondents' Club where the press was waiting for him. He looked refreshed and in good health. A condensation of his latest book, *The Night They Burned the Mountain,* had recently appeared in the July issue of our Japanese edition, and quite a few journalists representing foreign as well as Japanese newspapers and radio were on hand to meet him. Dooley gave an enthusiastic talk not only on his own medical work in Southeast Asia but also about his desire to enlist the support of the Japanese people and the active cooperation of Japanese doctors and nurses. He said that he was prepared to give talks anywhere in Japan where he was wanted because he was anxious to speak to the public and also to collect funds for his work. He suggested that people or organizations desiring to make lecture engagements could communicate with me at the *Reader's Digest* office in Tokyo.

Later, a number of schools and colleges in Kobe and Nara as well as organizations elsewhere in Japan wrote to me, but of course Tom Dooley was not destined to return.

In his lecture at the summer school he made a profound impression on the young social and medical workers who came to hear him. "We Medico workers," he said, "are neither missionaries nor government agents. We are human beings and doctors, and our sole purpose is to help our fellow human beings who need help. We believe that those who can afford to do so should help the poor, and that the healthy and strong should aid the sick, no matter what part of the world we come from or what part of the world they happen to be in." I made notes of this speech and reported it in Japanese in the monthly bulletin which is distributed to subscribers, and we received many responses from our readers.

I received one particularly interesting letter from a social worker who heard him that day. "Because Dr. Dooley is an American physician, we all expected him to discuss the latest developments of medical science in the U.S., and after the lecture someone asked a question along this line. Dr. Dooley's answer was what impressed me most. 'In a primitive country like Laos, where I operate, modern medical science has little meaning. Fancy laboratories and elaborate equipment hardly are appropriate when you even lack such basic things as electricity and running water. Our sick people need *basic* medicine, the kind of medicine that can be practiced in a mud hut or out of the doctor's kit bag. This may be primitive by most modern standards; but it is what the people need desperately, and it is all we can do under existing circumstances, and it is infinitely better than no medical service at all.' This, I believe, should be a sobering thought to Japanese medical workers who are forever seeking the new things."

During his visit to Tokyo he dined with the priests of St. Sophia University who are of various nationalities —French, German, Spanish, Japanese. But his host, Dr. John Blewett, is an American from St. Louis, Dooley's home town, and also an alumnus of St. Louis University. At dinner, Tom ate hardly anything, only some vegetable and a bit of fruit. When asked about his health, he said: "I think I shall live about six months, but not much more." This he said very calmly and serenely. After dinner they talked together for about an hour-and-a-half, and Tom said that he doubted he would be able to work in Laos for very long anyway. The Communists were spreading rumors among the natives that he was passing out poison and using drugs that made the natives go insane. He was not worried, he said, because his trained Lao nurses could keep up his work after him. His greatest concern, he said, was Medico's being able to continue the work he had started in Laos and elsewhere.

Later, Father Blewett and Tom strolled around St. Sophia House together reminiscing. Just then a group of students came out of the school building and were about to board a bus. Dooley spotted a couple of students who looked like Lao. He approached them and spoke to them in their native language. The boys were so surprised that they just stared at him, unable to speak. Then, when he said he had been in Laos, they asked, almost in unison, "Do you know Dr. Dooley?" Dooley seemed to cherish this question and he invited both boys to luncheon. The four of us went to luncheon next day at a *tempura* restaurant called Hanacho, which Dooley had patronized during his days as a naval doctor at Yokosuka. Every time he came up to Tokyo, he used to eat there. He was fond of the restaurateur and his household, and they now treasure an album of his pictures and signature. Dooley talked to the two Lao students warmly and as if he had known them all their lives. He discussed their future plans and the future of Laos. He spoke confidently and inspiringly, as though he felt a deep obligation to pass along something he deemed sacred in life.

As our three days in Tokyo drew to a close, I felt impelled, as a friend of four years' standing, to mention my anxiety about his state of health. I was really cherishing a secret hope that some miracle might happen, or some treatment might be found, that would enable Tom Dooley to live much longer than expected. However, what I received in reply to my inquiry was a shock for which I was hardly prepared.

"I might be able to live for five or six more years if I remained in a hospital bed under constant treatment," he said. "But I wouldn't want to live on such terms. That wouldn't be living; it would be vegetation. I want to go on working on my medical project for six months more, rather than spend the next six years dying." When I heard these words I could not speak. Words simply would not come to my lips.

*August 1-4.* The new teams for Quang Ngai (Vietnam) and Ban Houei Sai (Laos) assembled in Hong Kong. Robert W. Anderson, who was traveling with Dooley to get material for the 20th Century-Fox screen play based on Dooley's life, recalls that "this was the first time I was to see him in the role of the Pied Piper, loping along at the head of a caravan of scurrying followers. Later I was to see him in Muong Sing, trailed by laughing, adoring children wherever he went; this time it was the crew of new corpsmen and nurses who scurried along trying to keep pace with him."

Reggie Gordon, 23 years old, a former medical technician at New York's Polyclinic Hospital, who was headed for Quang Ngai, says: "During this time in Hong Kong, we would start the day by having breakfast with him at eight o'clock. Then we started shopping for the various supplies the teams needed. Dr. Tom would show us the best places to go and how to bargain to get the best prices and the biggest discounts. He would keep us on the go all day long, and I kept wishing I had been a track star in school. Someone commented that Dooley was supposed to be a dying man, and added: 'I would hate like hell to follow him around when he's well!' "

Terry Cotter describes one of these Hong Kong shopping expeditions:

There were representatives of three teams along. I guess about six of us in all, in addition to Dooley and Mr. Anderson or one of the doctors. We would invade one of those big British-type department stores in force; two or three hours later we would move on leaving a lot of exhausted and bewildered clerks behind us.

Dr. Dooley would wander up and down the aisles with the rest of us tagging along. "I'll take a dozen of these, four of those, two dozen red ones, etc.," he would say. The rest of us meanwhile were picking out particular items we thought we might need.

Occasionally there would be a huddle to discuss the wisdom of purchasing a particular item or model. Dr. Dooley would give us brief lectures on the value or usefulness of certain things based on his experience.

After one of these hectic days, he took us to dinner at the Foreign Correspondents Club. Besides the excellent cuisine, the view of Hong Kong was unobstructed by clouds or fog—one of Kong Kong's beautiful nights. During this dinner Jan and I first became aware that Dr. Dooley, despite the thousands of people he knew, was really a lonely man. He often referred to the people in the Muong Sing valley as his family, and I don't doubt that his feelings for them were deep and sincere. We can't remember the words he used that revealed this loneliness, but it was definitely there.

While in Hong Kong, Dooley conferred with a number of people about plans for Medico's International Eye Bank which would make corneal transplants available to restore the sight of blind people in Asia. The project later was placed under the direction of Dr. John Harry King, the Washington ophthalmologist who developed the vacuum dehydration process which makes possible the storage and shipment of eyes donated to U.S. eye banks. The Medico International Eye Bank now serves sixteen nations on all continents of the globe. He also spoke before the Hong Kong Lions Club. Then the group moved on to Bangkok for more shopping.

"We were staying at the Erawan Hotel in Bangkok," says Terry Cotter, "and we were still running our legs off on Dooley errands. After one of these daily forays, the group met at the hotel swimming pool to cool off. Dr. Dooley was sitting beside the pool when we arrived, and we asked him to join us for a swim. He refused saying that the scars from his operation would scare away most of the hotel's patrons. But, it was a pleasure he couldn't resist for long, and after some decision-weighing, he took a long, running dive into the middle of the pool, clothes and all. The plunge

149

obviously caused him some discomfiture, but he tried to conceal it. Indeed, he tucked his bad shoulder to one side and managed a few more dives before he quit."

Bob Anderson mentions Dooley's "boundless energy during this period. He didn't seem to be driving himself *more* than usual, he just always drove himself. He had a clear sense of mission, there is no doubt of that. But I certainly had no sense that I was traveling with a sick man.

"My first wife died of cancer, and perhaps for that reason Tom felt he could discuss his cancer with me. Of course, Tom had a continual need to be flippant about everything, so even when he talked of his illness he was rather casual. Anyone who has lived with cancer knows that one of the terrible aspects is 'not knowing when.' When Tom talked of his plans for the future, he often seemed to catch himself and he would add hastily, 'Of course, we're not talking in terms of years but of months.'"

On the evening of August 4, when Dooley returned to Laos, he was met at the Vientiane airport by Bob Burns, the same "fat, lovable Bob Burns, who worked for USIS and called himself 'just a typist in the army of the Lord.'" They had met in 1958 when Dooley first arrived in Vientiane with 32 tons of pharmaceuticals and equipment and no place to store them except

upon Hank Miller's front lawn. Bob Burns also had
been aboard the U.S. embassy plane sent to Muong
Sing in August 1959, to bring Dooley on the first leg
of the long and mysterious journey to the United
States. Tom Dooley, at the time, was unaware of the
real reason why he had been ordered home; and Bob
Burns was one of the very few people who knew that
Tom Dooley's trouble had been diagnosed as an incurable form of cancer.

Bob Burns recalls:

On the evening of August 4, 1960, when he returned
to Vientiane, we had an engagement to dine at the
Settha Palace Hotel. He seemed tired and distraught
that night, and I was surprised to see him with his arm
again in the black-silk sling which I had understood
he had abandoned. He would also occasionally cradle
that bad arm with his left hand and grimace with pain.
As we talked I suddenly realized that he had lost something that was essentially part of the Tom Dooley I had
always known. I couldn't say exactly what it was, but
he just was not the same man.

At dinner that night there was, of course, a great
deal of talk about the many dangers that beset Laos.
We were all aware that serious trouble was brewing
for the Royal Lao government. The elections in the previous April had seemingly gone well enough in the sense
that the Communists had failed to win a single seat in
the national assembly. The vote had also virtually
eliminated the pro-Communist element in Parliament
and had given new importance to the "young reformers." General Phoumi Nosavan had been largely re-

sponsible for this success; but, because of Western opposition to a military man, the King had chosen Tiao Somsanith, one of General Phoumi's civilian colleagues, as premier.

That night Tom insisted that Lao politics did not concern him in the slightest. His job, he said, was to get up north as quickly as he could and get his new hospital started at Ban Houei Sai.

"I came to Laos knowing that the Communists would take over the country sooner or later," he said. "I intend to remain in Laos until my work is finished, or until I am forced to leave."

Two weeks later, Bob Burns next saw Tom Dooley in Luang Prabang, the old capital of the kingdom. Events had reached a critical turning point in the history of Laos. On August 9th, an unknown 26-year-old commander of a Royal Lao parachute battalion, Captain Kong Le, had occupied Vientiane with a mere 700 troops while the government and military leaders were in Luang Prabang for the cremation ceremonies of the late king. Captain Kong Le's forces immediately called for a reconciliation with the Communist Pathet Lao and for the expulsion of the American military mission. A few days later the Communist radio in Hanoi, capital of North Vietnam, announced that the Pathet Lao were ready to join in a new Lao government which would oust all Americans.

Ted Werner, Tom's new pilot, was in Vientiane on the night of Kong Le's coup d'etat (August 9-10). Ted recalls:

I dashed out to the airport and, without any clearance or other formalities, I took off and flew the Piper Apache to Bangkok. There was no way for me to communicate with Dooley, who was in Muong Sing, and I could only hope that he would hear of my action through Bob Burns or some of the other people in the American Embassy.

My primary duty, as I saw it, was to get the airplane safely out of Vientiane, because it certainly would be confiscated by Captain Kong Le's rebels if they got the opportunity.

On August 19 a commercial plane that had been taken over by the army stopped at Muong Sing and Dooley somehow got aboard and went to Luang Prabang with no assurance that he would be able to get back to Muong Sing or anywhere outside the old capital. That afternoon I was able to get through to Bob Burns in Luang Prabang on the radio band assigned to the U.S. military mission and he told me Tom was there. I asked for orders and Tom relayed word for me to get to Luang Prabang somehow, but to avoid Vientiane by all means. "We need that plane."

I went to see young Puke Sarasin, son of Pote Sarasin, Secretary General of SEATO, and some other Thai friends that afternoon. They all assured me I was in trouble, which I already knew. Legally, I could only fly from Thailand to Luang Prabang by way of Vientiane, which probably would mean sacrificing the airplane. But, worse than that, Thailand wasn't authorizing *any* flights to Laos because of the civil war there.

However, after a lot of string-pulling by the Sarasins, and other influential Thais, our Medico airplane was given special status and the commanding general of the

153

Thailand Air Force in Bangkok gave me my clearance and I flew directly to Luang Prabang.

Tom's first order was to fly him back to Bangkok where he had urgent business connected with supplies for the Laos hospitals. He was also worried about communications with Medico in New York and with the families of people on the Medico teams in Laos. During this period there was no cable connection between Laos and the outside world except through Vientiane. Everything to and from the rest of Laos stopped right there. However, there had been one amusing exception: Tom did receive one cable from 20th Century-Fox asking if Frank Sinatra or Jack Lemmon would be acceptable for the lead in the Tom Dooley film! This one cable came through to Luang Prabang promptly and in perfect English, which was exceptional also. The rebel censors must have been impressed by the names of the movie stars.

*September 1-3.* On the first day of September Ted Werner flew Dooley across the South China Sea to Kuala Lumpur, capital of the Federation of Malaya, where an agreement had been drawn between the local government and Medico for operation of a hospital. That evening Tom Dooley dined with Dr. Dato Ong Yoke Lin, Malaya's Minister of Health, and the report he later sent to New York was exultant. Dooley wrote:

Dato Ong and his staff worked over the agreement for the hospital which is located at Kuala Lipis, a village which is in the state of Pahang and about 110 miles from the capital. Malaya is a federation of 11 states, and each state has a sultan or raja of its own. The Sultan of Pahang will be the titular head of our Medico team.

Malaya, I think, is going to be a good example of how Medico tailors each program to fit the needs of the particular nation.

The Sultan of Pahang has built a fine network of roads through the jungles of central Malaya, and his people can come from all around the jungle to this central area. Rather than ask Medico to build a village hospital, such as we have at Muong Sing or Ban Houei Sai, they have asked us to take over an existing hospital, enlarge it, build a modern operating room, and install a modern X-ray unit. We've been asked to convert this hospital into a small medical center. We will bring in a team of doctors, nurses and technicians and, in addition to treating patients, we will also start a training program for Malayan personnel.

The next morning (September 2) we took off in a small airplane belonging to the Malayan Air Force and, after a short flight of about thirty minutes, we landed on the airstrip of a big rubber estate, where a car picked us up and drove us to Kuala Lipis, which is another twenty minutes away. Kuala Lipis is only a small town, but it is the center of a larger area with a population of about forty thousand people. The present hospital has two Malayan doctors on the staff and four nurses. They have an out-patient sick call of about 100 people every day, and they can accommodate about 130 patients in the wards.

Our first job will be to modernize the operating room,

since the present one is nothing more than what we would call a good dressing room. Kuala Lipis has electricity and running water so there is no problem there. We will need one general doctor, one surgeon, an X-ray technician, a laboratory technician and three general nurses. The physician can be a married man because this is a nice, clean town with good living accommodations.

I flew back to Kuala Lumpur, and had lunch with the Prime Minister and with several members of the Cabinet, as well as Dato Ong Yoke Lin. The King of Malaya is seriously ill and is not expected to live, so the luncheon was rather small and subdued. Now the most important thing is for you to screen our lists and choose one top-notch doctor (or perhaps two) and the required nurses and technicians. I would like to have them out here within the next month or six weeks.

*September 5-16.* Dooley made the rounds of the new hospitals. Ban Houei Sai in Laos and Quang Ngai in Vietnam to see how the new teams were operating before settling down in Muong Sing where he knew problems awaited. He was delighted with Quang Ngai which Dr. Carl Wiedermann had taken over during the preceding month.

Dr. Wiedermann had been born in Germany, educated in Italy, and had received his medical degree from the University of Naples, before coming to the U. S. for graduate training in 1954. "He is a wonderful blend of the finest in the Old World and the best in America," Tom Dooley said. "To understand him, think of a man who likes to relax after a 14-16 hour day by playing seventeenth century chamber music on a battery-driven record player."

Dr. Wiedermann's respect for Tom Dooley, as well as his critical view of Dooley's shortcomings, had grown also since they left the States. Says Carl Wiedermann:

I found Tom Dooley fairly easy to get along with. Despite what I had heard from others, he was perfectly willing to have you disagree with his suggestions. He always said he didn't want a "yes man" around. On the contrary, he said: "I don't want to hear what you think is going well. I want to hear what you think is *not* going well. I want to hear your criticisms. I don't want to hear any flattering things." And I never told him any flattering things, never. Dooley, however, was a stern disciplinarian. He felt that he was the captain of the team and in complete charge of the program. He expected complete obedience from his corpsmen and nurses. In this you could recognize his Navy background. Personally, I am completely anti-militaristic. I try to work things out with my own team on a kind of general discussion basis. Sometimes Tom Dooley would criticize me for this. He would say: "You simply must give the orders, and they must obey."

When he was in charge, he knew every detail of what was going on. He knew how much sugar was needed for a month's or six months' supply, and the amount of gasoline needed for the old jeep. He was a meticulous housekeeper in addition to being a good doctor.

And, incidentally, Tom Dooley was a *good doctor*. He didn't have much time for pre-operative or post-operative care, but he was a good diagnostician and he did good therapy. He was an all-round doctor. He knew the latest treatment for malaria, for example, or the amoebic diseases. He had brushed up on his tropical medicine and other specialties. He read not only journals of general medicine but also the specialized journals. He had his books on ophthalmology, for example, and he would read them. He was always interested in acquiring new instruments like special clamps to get polyps out of the nose or the latest system for giving anesthesia. He was a *good* doctor, and obviously interested in his job.

He had a chip on his shoulder because he was considered a "jungle doctor" and he had made it almost a challenge. He would say: "I *am* a jungle doctor and I am practicing nineteenth century medicine." But he left it up to his colleagues and associates to find out that he really was doing an excellent job under difficult conditions. I was very much impressed.

Al Harris who was one of the two corpsmen at Quang Ngai also testifies that Tom Dooley had a "top-sergeant type of personality." Says Harris: "Many times I have heard Dr. Dooley say that in any group someone has to be in absolute command or the group will perish. He once told me that the person in command always ends up being hated by the others. 'But,' he said, 'that's the price of leadership.' He cited the example of two groups of Americans who were taken prisoner by the Communists. One group did as they pleased, but in the second group one man took command and told the others when and what to eat, when and how to exercise, etc. The first group went to pieces; the other group survived."

Harris' team-mate, Reggie Gordon, felt the sting of Dooley's tongue-lashings several times. Says Gordon:

Dr. Tom could drive you out of your mind with his sarcastic remarks, and his constant nagging. He would always say, "My way is best until you can prove me wrong, so I want things done my way." Dr. Dooley and I never got along too well. One of his pet peeves was my instinctive use of the word "yep" instead of "yes, sir." If he asked me a question and I replied "yep" he would always ask, "What did you say?" I didn't do this to make him mad; it was just a habit and I would forget myself when we were busy. One time he said, "I wish I had you with me in Muong Sing for one month. I'd teach you to say, 'Yes, sir' and 'no, sir.'"

On one of his visits to Quang Ngai, he made me hate him with all the passion of hell! I was determined to leave Medico. We had been in Quang Ngai only a short time and we were all tired and depressed and our nerves were on edge. We were doing an operation and Dr. Tom administered the anesthesia. He got on my back because I was wearing work clothes in the operating room. I told him I didn't have a cap and gown to wear. He kept nagging and cutting me down throughout the operation, until I felt just about two inches tall. After the operation, he handed me some cloth and said, "Now make yourself a gown and keep it clean and don't ever let me see you come in here again with those clothes on." Oh, how I hated him at that time!

Dr. Dooley never told you when you had done something well. He always told you what *should* have been done. He said to me one day, "I never tell a person what he has done well because if he has done a good job he knows it. My job is to tell them when they're not right so that they'll never repeat their errors."

In Muong Sing Dr. Ronald Wintrob had taken over and his dislike of Tom Dooley seemed to become intensified. He considered Dooley egotistical, obstinate, and overbearing.

Dr. Wintrob wanted a decent chair (a reasonable enough request in view of Dooley's Spartan taste for packing-case furniture) and apparently had purchased one in Vientiane. Dooley refused to have the chair brought to Muong Sing; he said the airplane's limited capacity was needed for more essential cargo. Dooley's memos to New York, however, indicated that he liked Ronald Wintrob and had respect for him as a doctor. Apart from the clashing of two strong personalities, apparently matters of authority and discipline were involved.

Dr. Wintrob wore a beard and Dooley insisted that the beard must come off. "I have tried to make Ronny understand that in Indochina a beard still marks a white man as a Frenchman and the people here still despise the French colonials. But he says he has worn a beard since he was in medical school and has no intention of shaving now. He was clearly bucking my authority, so I told him to make up his mind: either shave it off or take his plane ticket and go home. (The beard came off.)"

Dr. Wintrob adds: "The intense dislike I felt for Tom melted a little over the next few months. As he realized I was running his hospital as well as he could have wished, he became more tolerant of my opinions and less impatient. I did not change my opinion of Tom's character and motivations, but I did become slightly more tolerant of the probable depth of sincerity which he had lost in proportion to his increasing fame."

*September 21-30.* Vientiane, beleaguered capital of Laos, was in chaos when Dooley arrived there on September 21. General Phoumi's forces were still threatening to destroy the central part of the city where the public buildings are located. The waterworks and power station had been bombed leaving part of the city without water or electricity. Virtually no gasoline was available. Because Vientiane imports everything from Thailand across the Mekong River, the blockade or embargo (for which both the Lao Royal government and the government of Thailand disclaimed responsibility) had left the city virtually without food, drugs, fuel and other essentials.

Dooley found himself caught up in a bad situation. Medico's supplies of pharmaceuticals as well as much of the equipment for the new hospital in Ban Houei

Sai were all tied up in the customs warehouse in Bangkok, Thailand. Normally, these could be moved under
bond into Laos, with which Medico has an agreement
waiving import duties. But because of the blockade
nothing was moving through regular channels. The
alternative was to smuggle the huge cargo into Laos
(which was what Tom Dooley had in mind); but in
order to do this he would have to take possession of
the stuff in Thailand. And Medico operated no program in Thailand and had no import agreement with
the Thai government—"which is pretty sticky about
import duties, from which they derive more revenue
than the entire national budget," Dooley reminded the
New York office. On the supplies he needed at the
moment for the hospitals in Cambodia and Laos alone
he would have to pay Thailand import duties amount-
ing to $65,000.

As usual, he had influential friends in the right
places. He went to Bangkok to see Pote Sarasin, former
ambassador of Thailand to the United Nations and
head of SEATO, and asked for the release of Medico's
supplies duty free.

"You are asking for the impossible—as usual," Pote
Sarasin told him. "But I'll think it over. Come back
and see me tomorrow."

Next day, Pote Sarasin told him that the matter had
been discussed with several cabinet ministers and the
Chief of Customs. The consensus was that no one
could waive the duties but the King himself, and he

was in Sweden at the moment. However, Pote Sarasin thought the Prime Minister, Marshal Sarit, might be able to help.

"Fine. How do I get to see him?"

"I knew you would ask that," Sarasin smiled. "You have an appointment with the Prime Minister at four o'clock this afternoon."

Dooley reported to New York later: "Marshal Sarit was most kind, but I had a tough time selling him. Finally, he was persuaded that the humanitarian concepts which Medico represents, were beyond consideration of war and politics, and in my presence he ordered the chief of customs to release our supplies. He attached only one condition: "Please don't sell any of that stuff in Thailand or you will upset our budget."

In New York, Tom Regan, in charge of supplies for Medico's overseas installations, heaved a sigh of relief when he heard that Dooley had pried loose the embargoed shipments without having to pay a budget-busting $65,000 in customs duties. "Quite aside from the valuable equipment for Ban Houei Sai," Regan says, "we really were in desperate need of pharmaceuticals in Muong Sing and Ban Houei Sai. But now that Dr. Tom had everything in his possession in Bangkok, the big question was how did he intend to get the supplies into northern Laos. We suspected that he had a bit of smuggling or illegal border-crossing in mind, and we were on tenterhooks for the next week or so."

How Tom Dooley pulled off this small miracle of

163

logistics can be pieced together from his own terse reports, and those of Tom Kirby and Terry Cotter, plus the recollections of Tom Regan. Young Tom Kirby was summoned to Bangkok where the 16 tons of supplies were loaded into several boxcars of the little narrow-gauge railway which runs up to the northern tip of Thailand. Kirby traveled with the shipment to the end of the line at the town of Chiang Rai. There the crates were transferred to a motley caravan of ox carts and broken-down trucks and carried overland to the town of Chiang Khong on the Mekong River.

Meanwhile Terry Cotter had been ordered to leave Ban Houei Sai and round up every available barge, pirogue and canoe along the river and to assemble his flotilla at Chiang Khong. There he met up with Tom Kirby, the cargo was loaded aboard some twenty-five small craft and floated down to Ban Houei Sai on the Laos shore of the Mekong.

"From Ban Houei Sai, Muong Sing's supplies had to be lifted by plane," says Tom Regan, "and we knew there was practically no more gasoline available in Laos. But when Doctor Tom arrived a few days later he had the Piper Apache's tanks full and a reserve tank aboard. We never did find out how he did it, but the whole operation went off without a hitch. After that, the boys called Tom 'Old Smuggler.' It was an incredible maneuver for anyone to bring off so successfully, but I think it was downright heroic for a man as sick as Tom must have been at that time."

# PART FIVE

## 1960:

## FALL

*October 7-28.* Dooley returned to New York early in October to undergo his second series of tests at Memorial and to attend the Medico board meeting. He told everyone that the results of the tests again were negative. This was gratifying news which convinced many of his lay friends that a miracle had occurred and led even some of the doctors to say hopefully that perhaps Tom Dooley "had the thing beaten." Yet as the date of the Medico board meeting (October 15) approached, he seemed depressed, irritable, restless. He told friends that "it looks as though I'll have to come back to the States after January and come back this time to stay." Because there was no evidence of any physical setback, his friends attributed this intention to come back to Dooley's dissatisfaction with Medico's management and to his desire to assume direction personally.

However, this assumption is not supported by Medico's status at the time nor by Dooley's letters and memoranda on the subject. He was impatient with the

167

slowness of the personnel recruiting program and he would have liked to have seen Medico expand activities at an even faster rate. He also complained that too much of the fund-raising activities was borne by him alone. Earlier in the year he had stated in a long memo (Re: Suggestions for the Operation of Medico) to Paul Hellmuth: "I do not like Medico to be so dependent on me and my personality. . . . I do not think the foundation should be built upon such shifting sands."

Leo Cherne, executive director of the Research Institute of America, advances an interesting theory regarding Tom Dooley's thinking at the time. Dooley and Leo Cherne had met while Medico was still a subsidiary of the International Rescue Committee. They became fast friends and their friendship remained unimpaired by Dooley's decision to separate Medico from IRC.

Leo Cherne says:

When Tom came to see me in October 1960, after having been here for a check-up, he came for the purpose of exploring his doubts and fortifying his convictions. There was no question at all in Tom's mind that in Medico there had been constructed an instrument which was a multiplication of his vision and, without any question, a multiplication of the only thing he thought genuinely useful—at least within the frame of reference of his capacities. He had no doubts about this. He had no significant doubts about the future of

Medico, its function, its purpose. But he began to mani-
fest some anxiety about the sheer size and complexity
of the organization itself.

In a sense, organization—the larger, more impersonal
thing—is the very opposite of what was at the very
heart of Tom Dooley in a tiny village in Laos where
the essence is simplicity. In Nam Tha or Muong Sing
there were no intermediaries between the hand and the
wound.

So, in October, he not only returned with the dis-
couragement of his own year of physical trial, but also
he was torn between a contradiction that perhaps cannot be resolved—between his dream of Dooley-like,
Schweitzer-like operations all over the world wherever
they are needed that would nevertheless remain at their
very essence direct and simple and uncomplicated.

Tom was additionally concerned because on his return in the fall of 1960, he was now witnessing, as a
result of an admiring nation's response to his own physical courage, a gargantuan thing—wealthy in its re-
sources, ambitious in its undertakings, and extremely
complicated in its operation. He wondered if Medico
was slipping away from his original concept.

For this same reason, at the time of his operation in
1959 when he first faced the possibility of death, Tom
had readily understood and accepted advice which suggested separating Medico from IRC, because it seemed
to him that he was separating something that was direct
and personal and still small from something larger, with
its complex of fund-raising and office staff. He thought
then that Medico would go back to simple beginnings.

Now, in October 1960, he really came to see me because he discovered that he hadn't solved that problem

at all, that in its turn, largely because of his own efforts and his own genius, Medico now had become a large complex apparatus—even larger and more complex than the one he had divorced himself from in the fall of 1959.

At the board meeting on October 15 Tom Dooley was elected vice-chairman of Medico. He seemed satisfied with the way things were shaping up. "Within the next few weeks," he said, "I am going to New Delhi to open up a new program for the Tibetan refugees, then to Afghanistan and Malaya. After these activities get under way, we want to have a period of consolidation in Medico. We must not make the mistake of over-reaching ourselves. We must not make the mistake of having a lot of half-launched projects that sink before they even get out of the harbor. We also must have a new organizational set-up which is much less dependent upon one man—Dooley."

Between October 18 and 28 he gave talks and attended meetings in San Francisco, St. Louis and Toronto; then, on October 28th he took a plane at New York International Airport to India. He extracted a promise from Malcolm Dooley and Bob Copenhaver that they would visit him in Asia the following month and not in the spring of 1961, as Copenhaver would have preferred. He said enigmatically. "Come in November or not at all. I won't be out there after January."

170

*October 30-31.* The telephone rang in the office of Dr. Melvin A. Casberg, dean of the Christian Medical College, in Ludhiana, a city in the northern Punjab part of India. The operator in Delhi announced that Dr. Jungalwalla, Deputy Director General of Health, was on the line.

"Dr. Casberg, we have an offer from Dr. Tom Dooley of Medico to help the Tibetan refugees on our Northern Frontier. The project is a simple one—medicines, equipment and vehicles for a roving medical team. Knowing that you are a personal friend of Dr. Dooley's and also on his Medical Advisory Board I wonder if you could give us some information and assistance in this matter?"

Dr. Casberg said that he would be glad to help, and added that he had recently received a letter from Dooley, written in Rangoon, expressing a desire to visit Delhi and Ludhiana to discuss the matter.

As I put down the phone my mind raced back to my first meeting with Tom Dooley. The year was 1949; the place was the Gold Room of the Jefferson Hotel in St. Louis where a dinner was being held in honor of my inauguration as Dean of St. Louis University School of Medicine. Barely audible in the chatter of a thousand voices and the clattering of dishes, an informal piano recital was being given on the stage at the end of the big ballroom. The pianist was Tom Dooley.

Tom, as a medical student, showed evidence of his dynamic energy in ways which were not always appreciated by those responsible for the administration of

171

the university. Schedules of clinics and class attendance are a necessary part of organized instruction; but Tom chafed under certain of these rigid restrictions to the extent that instead of attending required classes he often became absorbed in unscheduled medical activities. The faculty reaction to such unorthodoxy made it necessary for Tom to meet me occasionally in the Dean's office. Even at this stage of his development I recognized a heart which could not be restrained within the boundaries of the routine things of life. These early meetings of Tom Dooley, the student, with me the Dean developed into a friendship which continued to draw us closer through the ensuing years.

The next stage in this friendship came about with Tom's graduation from Medical College and his desire to serve his country. In the interim my duties changed from St. Louis to Washington, D.C., where I had been appointed Assistant Secretary of Defense (Health and Medical). Tom then was in the Navy and on one of my trips to the West Coast I stopped at the Naval Hospital at Camp Pendleton, California, on a routine inspection of the personnel and facilities.

At the hospital over a cup of coffee I asked the commanding officer how Tom Dooley was doing as a member of his staff.

"'Dooley is certainly *different,*' he said cautiously. 'He has boundless energy, but I must say that he utilizes his energy in the most unorthodox ways. This relates not to a willful desire to upset routine but rather to his becoming completely absorbed in a project to the loss of his sense of responsibility to other related areas.' Obviously, time, experience, and discipline had not changed him.

172

Later, when I had retired from the Defense Department, and was settled in California as a practicing surgeon, Tom drove up to our home one afternoon, unbuckled the seat belt and jumped out of his flashy red convertible without even opening the door. The gleam in his eye told me that he was off on some new adventure.

"Sir, I've been ordered to Japan," he said standing erect before me, his face wreathed in that captivating Irish smile. Tom always addressed me as "Sir," a hangover from the days when I was his Dean. Following that brief visit, he drove north to San Francisco, where he embarked for duty in the Far East.

Letters began to arrive from across the Pacific. As the correspondence focused on his activities in North Vietnam, it was evident that Tom had been shaken to the very depths of his being. There came an awakening to the desperate needs of people in that part of the world. I knew then that Tom would never be the same carefree young man again. The story of his transformation was vividly told in his book, *Deliver Us From Evil.*

I next saw Tom at the National Airport in Washington where I had been attending a meeting of a medical defense committee. We ran into each other in the airport dining room and then, as my plane departure was announced, Tom followed me aboard the plane and sat on the arm of my seat. The "No Smoking" and "Fasten Seat Belt" signs flashed on, but that made little difference to Tom, who was engrossed in a discussion of his future plans. Eventually the stewardess almost dragged him off the plane, much to the amusement of the other passengers. The big question in Tom's mind was, "How can I do the most with my life for those in

173

Southeast Asia who have so little?" Deluged with advice, his mind was in a state of confusion. It was evident that his heart would never be satisfied without an opportunity to serve his newly found friends in Asia. I urged him to follow his heart.

My wife's brother, Dr. William Van Valin, a California surgeon, was in the Far East in 1959, and at my request he flew up and spent a few days in Tom's jungle hospital in northern Laos. The story of the removal of the cancerous lymph gland by Dr. Van Valin is now a matter of history. Now, by strange coincidence, on Saturday, October 29, 1960, I received a telephone call from Bill Van Valin who, with his wife, Pauli, just arrived in Delhi. They wanted to come up to spend a few days with us here at Ludhiana. Unknown to them our mutual friend Tom also was arriving in Delhi by plane the next morning. I had made arrangements for a car to drive him the 180 miles to our home. Thus a most unusual coincidence brought together the Van Valins and Tom Dooley as guests in our home, with neither party even knowing that the other was in India.

The two days passed rapidly. Tom alternated between resting and unburdening his heart in relation to the challenges of Medico. It was quite evident that he was suffering but equally evident that he was refusing to bow to this handicap.

On the afternoon of his arrival in Ludhiana, at short notice I called together the student body of our medical school, and Tom, in his usual fashion, won their hearts with his earnestness, Irish wit and challenge. One incident of his association with my students, I learned from them only after Tom had left. At their request, he spent an evening in the men's dormitory discussing interna-

174

tional health problems. Later they joined in song, and Dooley asked the students if they had ever serenaded the ladies' dormitory. The fact that this was unheard of in the Punjab made no difference to Tom. Within a few moments he rounded up the boys and led them in serenading the ladies' dormitory, much to the delight of all the students, and especially the surprised ladies.

Mrs. Casberg and I brought a Hammond electric organ with us to India, and on the night before he left, Tom gave us a memorable evening of relaxation. For almost an hour, we sat back and listened to Tom play the organ. He appeared to be lost in another world, one of memories. We conversed in the language of music—praying for him as he played the stirring chords of Ave Maria, and then tapping our feet to the lilting Irish tunes which danced from his fingertips. When he finished playing he lay down on the floor, exhausted, a pillow under his head, and closed his eyes with a deep sigh. Bill Van Valin and I knew that his body ached with the pain of spreading cancer.

Tom was aware that his time was short and this only added fuel to his energy and drove him even more furiously in an effort to help those less fortunate. That night, after our music session, Tom took me into the bedroom, removed his shirt, asked me to check his chest. I examined the scars and felt carefully for evidence of a spreading cancer. There were no objective signs of a recurrence, but the pain in his back and other subjective symptoms told us both that the melanoma had not been eradicated. During the evening I had noticed how he often stretched backwards and then gripped his waist with both hands in an effort to squeeze out the pain.

175

As Tom put on his shirt covering the marks of surgery, I saw beyond these scars to the beatings he had received in Laos. The physical deformities were badges earned in a courageous battle against the suffering and poverty of his friends in Asia. Tom had taken to heart the admonition that every man is indeed his brother's keeper.

On the night of October 31, I drove Tom to the railway station at Ludhiana and placed him on the Frontier Mail headed back for Delhi. A large number of students gathered on the platform to wish him farewell. Tom stood at the door of the coach and once more led them in singing. Before the train left I climbed aboard into the compartment and, shaking Tom's hand, wished him God's blessings. As we looked into each other's eyes, both of us knew that we would not see each other again in this life.

*November 2-5.* In New Delhi, Dooley conferred with Dr. Acharya Kripalani, chairman of the Central Relief Committee for Tibetans, and agreed that Medico would furnish a large jeep-truck to serve as a mobile medical unit and a smaller jeep for transporting personnel to serve the Tibetan refugees in the northern Punjab region. The project was to be managed by an independent Central Indian Committee composed of Madame Pandit Nehru, Dr. Kripalani, Dr. Melvin Casberg and the Vice President of India, Dr. Radhakrishman. The doctors and nurses attached to the unit were to be Sikhs recruited from among the graduates of the Christian Medical College in Ludhiana.

While he was in New Delhi he spent some time with E. F. (Gerry) Gerold, Jr., director of Pan American World Airways in India.

I took Tom around on the "Delhi Circuit," the endless rat-race that goes on in diplomatic and social circles in the Indian capital [Gerry Gerold writes]. I wanted him to meet as many people as possible—and that he did. One evening we attended a reception given by the German Ambassador for the former President of the West German Republic, Dr. Theodor Heuss, where Tom met many of my friends, including Dr. Radhakrishman, the Vice President of India. At that same gathering I introduced Tom to the Consul General of South Vietnam—who practically fainted from surprise when Dr. Dooley started conversing in Vietnamese! And it was the same when he spoke to a member of the French Embassy staff in fluent French.

From the German Embassy we moved on to the Vatican Legation where a reception was being held to celebrate the anniversary of the Coronation of Pope John XXIII. Here Tom was really the center of attention and, I'm afraid, he somewhat dimmed the glamor of the crimson-robed archbishops, bishops, monsignori— eighty-five in all! Yet they crowded around Tom asking question after question—and getting all the answers. But the clergy had ample competition there also—because many lovely diplomatic wives were in the throng, elbowing their way in to get a bit of the Dooley charm.

The day before his departure I asked him if he could possibly spare a half hour to have tea with the sisters at the Holy Family Hospital, a new and thriving American-type hospital in New Delhi, since many of the nuns were from the States. He readily agreed—and that "tea party" was a social event I shall never forget. There were fourteen nuns in their starchy white habits seated in front of us, literally hanging on every word Tom uttered. Here was a knowing audience. These dedicated women spoke and understood Dr. Dooley's language. He told them about his own hospital in "his" village and amusingly compared his hospital with theirs.

Although Tom had discussed his illness with me privately, this was the first time I ever heard him discuss it with anyone else. Since these sisters were professional nurses, he told them all about the nature of his cancer, described the operation which had taken place in 1959, and answered technical questions concerning his condition. He summed up by saying: "As you all know, I should have been dead a year ago. I should not really be here, and I know I can't go on forever. But I have so much to do, all I ask is your prayers."

I can tell you there were fifteen pairs of moist eyes— including my own—in the room on that November evening. The scheduled half hour lasted almost two hours! And I have never seen a more pleased and appreciative audience. Since that evening those Sisters have never ceased remembering Tom in their prayers.

The first time I noticed anything bothering Tom was when we started up the hospital stairs to visit the Chapel. He appeared to be having some difficulty making the steps—as though that slight limp had grown worse. Nothing was said at the time, but when we were in the car driving back to the city I asked him if his leg was bothering him. He said there was always some pain there but it was merely an aftermath of the skin graft done at the time of his operation. Then it suddenly

178

occurred to me that he did look tired and drawn. But I thought, Who wouldn't be tired? He has been on the run constantly. And when he wasn't on the run, he was dictating to his little machine or typing letters, or making telephone calls, or keeping appointments! As I wrote to my parents at the time, "Tom may have had cancer, but he is a real human dynamo!"

Dooley's (and Medico's) interest in the plight of the Tibetan refugees in northern India was a direct outgrowth of his friendship with Travis L. Fletcher, field director of the American Emergency Committee for Tibetan Refugees, and a veteran of American relief work in the Far East. Travis Fletcher tells the story:

Late in August 1956, while I was representing the organization Aid Refugee Chinese Intellectuals (ARCI), I returned to Hong Kong from a trip to Laos where I had gone for the purpose of placing Chinese doctors, engineers, accountants and other intellectual refugees in jobs with American missions operating in that beleaguered country. Despite many handicaps, officials of ICA in Vientiane were making efforts to organize, construct temporary buildings and recruit personnel. They were in desperate need of personnel with knowledge of French and English. Among Chinese refugees in Hong Kong there were hundreds with these qualifications.

On the morning after my return to Hong Kong I read in the English-language newspaper a front-page story about young Dr. Tom Dooley who was staying in the same hotel on his way to Laos to establish a hospital in the jungle. It immediately occurred to me that he might be able to use some of our refugee doctors. I put in a telephone call to Dr. Dooley's room and in a moment a crisp voice answered: "This is Dr. Dooley, what can I do for you?"

I explained that I had just returned from Laos and that I was anxious to resettle some of the thousands of intellectuals, including doctors, who were then stranded in Hong Kong, their talents being wasted because of the lack of opportunity. His reply came quickly over the telephone, "I would like to see you but I am leaving tomorrow morning and my day is practically filled. I will call you back if I can find time. What is your number?" I explained that I was living in the Miramar; that I was going to the U. S. Consulate General that morning, but would be available during the remainder of the day. I introduced myself in this way because by that time Dr. Dooley had become a celebrity, and celebrities are wary of telephone calls from strangers.

Ten minutes later, the telephone rang and it was Tom Dooley again. "I am sorry for my abrupt manner when you called. I know who you are now." He suggested that we have lunch together.

Thus it was that I first came to know Dr. Dooley. At lunch he began by telling of his experiences in evacuating refugees from North Vietnam. I had read the condensation of his book *Deliver Us From Evil* in the Reader's Digest and I was able, therefore, to follow his conversation. It was quite evident that Dr. Dooley liked to talk, and I like to talk, so the luncheon developed into something of a sparring match. Anyone who has met with Dr. Dooley on this basis will realize that the odds were against me! But I fought on, and he became as interested in what I was doing as I was in his program.

Dr. Dooley was deeply interested in the fact that the chairman and guiding influence in our organization, ARCI, was Dr. Walter H. Judd, U. S. Congressman from Minnesota. Dr. Judd is one of the few medical doctors in Congress, and Dr. Dooley revealed that he had talked with him in Washington to seek his advice about his own program in Laos.

Lunch went on for over two hours. At first it was "Dr. Dooley" and "Mr. Fletcher," but it was not long before it was "Travis" and "Tom." We soon were fast friends.

I told Tom of my desire to place qualified people in work in Laos where they would be useful to our mission and a help to the people of Laos. We had already been requested by the ICA during my visit to Laos, to recommend accountants, engineers and others. Dr. Dooley was rather doubtful as to whether it would be desirable to employ Chinese doctors in his hospital there, so near the Chinese Communist border, because as he said, "I would not want to be responsible for their heads, if and when the Chinese Communists found out that they were Chinese who *opposed* Communism." He expressed a desire, however, to help in placing these refugees, and promised to give his full support.

Three weeks later Dr. Dooley was back in Hong Kong to ask my help in purchasing supplies. He explained the difficulty in getting supplies up to the jungle area that he had selected as the site of his hospital. He was discouraged by the handicap and failures in his early attempts to get the cooperation he needed in Laos. To people who have spent years in the Orient this was understandable. In this part of the world there is a lack of respect for youth. Gray hair, or none at all, is an asset. This is a pleasant revelation to those past forty-five, but it was a severe handicap to Dr. Dooley at the outset. That he overcame the handicap of his youth in a short time with the people of Laos and other Asians is a tribute to the character and personality of this young man. Overcoming all of the hardships and with the assistance of young, dedicated men, Dr. Dooley did establish his little hospital in the northern jungle of Laos and gained the admiration generally of people throughout the world.

On this trip to Hong Kong a dinner was arranged so that he could meet members of the medical profession who were later to become so enthusiastic about his program and whom he numbered among his closest friends during the last years of his life.

As Christmas approached in 1956 I was surprised one day to receive from Dr. Dooley a check for $500 asking me to dole this out to his three assistants who were coming to Hong Kong at his expense for a well earned vacation from the jungle. "If I give them this money, Travis, they will spend it all the first day, just as I would. You must handle the money during the few days they are there to keep a check-rein on them." But at the close of the letter there was a contradictory postscript that read, "If they need more, give it to them, I will reimburse you."

The young assistants Norm Baker, Pete Kessey and Dennis Shepard came to my office a few days later and we began the "dole." For three young men in Hong Kong after a year in the Laos jungle $500 was not enough. It was nearer $750, but Dr. Dooley had his reward in the devotion and dedication of these young men to an extent that one rarely observes.

In the following months, Dr. Dooley made many trips to Hong Kong and I saw him twice in Laos. He was constantly talking of an organization of dedicated doctors and nurses from America who would render a service to the underdeveloped areas of the world, and in any place where there was a concentration of distressed people. Many times he said, "No one gets as close to a person as his doctor, and it is on a close person-to-person basis that we must demonstrate our sincerity and devotion to the things for which America stands. The medical profession is in an excellent position to do this."

One day in the summer of 1959 I was in my office in Hong Kong interviewing Chinese applicants seeking positions in our missions in Laos.

The telephone rang, and I lifted the receiver to hear an American voice say, "Mr. Fletcher, this is Dr. Van Valin. I am at the Astor Hotel and I have just come from Laos. I have a letter for you from your friend Tom Dooley." I had other appointments so suggested that we might have lunch together the next day. The voice was insistent, however, "No, Mr. Fletcher, I must see you immediately. It is not just the letter. It is something much more important and I would like to talk with you." There was a note of anxiety in his voice so I concluded my interview and left for the Astor Hotel to meet him.

When Dr. Van Valin handed me the letter and I began to open it he impatiently said, "No, please Mr. Fletcher, let me first tell you some bad news." Then he related how he and Tom Dooley had been friends and how on Tom's invitation he had gone to Laos to spend his vacation in Muong Sing. While there he had noticed a lump on Tom's side, the appearance of which did not please him. He had persuaded Tom to let him remove it surgically, and even then as he observed the tissue he became suspicious. He explained that he had preserved a specimen of the tissue and had submitted it to a laboratory in Bangkok. There a pathological examination had revealed it to be a melanoma, a very malignant type of cancer.

"Knowing that you and Tom are such good friends," Dr. Van Valin said, "I would like your thoughts on what should be our next move."

In a situation like this it is impossible to gauge the effect that knowledge of having cancer might have on a patient. This is a moot question, even among doctors. As a layman, therefore, I suggested that we call Dr. Peter Comanduras of Medico in New York.

Dr. Van Valin had trouble in getting the call through, but when the news was related to Dr. Comanduras it was decided that a cable would be sent to Tom ordering him to return to New York immediately. As Tom explained in his next book, *The Night They Burned the Mountain,* he actually learned of his condition before he left Laos from a close friend, Hank Miller, then the head of the USIS [U.S. Information Service] in Laos.

Unfortunately I had to be away from Hong Kong when Tom came through there on his way to America, but I followed the story of Tom's surgery through the press and shortwave radio as did thousands of his friends. Shortly after the operation I had a long letter from him written in New York about Medico and of his plans to establish medical teams around the world.

Meanwhile, ARCI had resettled 15,000 Chinese in-

tellectuals throughout the world and had contributed
to the rehabilitation of hundreds more in Hong Kong.
I felt that the time had come for me to bow out, and
so informed Dr. Judd.

About that time word came out of India that the
Chinese Communists had invaded Lhasa and that the
Dalai Lama himself was attempting to escape to India.
For several days the world waited anxiously to hear of
his fate, and then the Dalai Lama did miraculously escape to India with approximately 10,000 of his followers.

I was about to leave Hong Kong to return to America
when I received a phone call from America asking me
to stop in India to ascertain the true situation as to the
number of Tibetans who had fled there, and to what
extent friends of the Tibetan people in America might
help in this tragedy. I was asked to report my findings
to Mr. Lowell Thomas, who was organizing a committee to help the Tibetan refugees.

As I prepared to leave Hong Kong for India, I received a call, and a familiar voice greeted me from
Bangkok. It was Tom Dooley saying that he had heard
that I was to go to India and asking if there was some
way that the Medico organization could help. I told
him that I was a complete novice as far as India was
concerned and I would let him know as soon as I could
get the facts for myself and Mr. Thomas.

Once the picture was clear a cable was dispatched to
Mr. Thomas, the longest one I had ever sent, asking him
to appeal to the American people for help for the Tibetans. My preliminary observations convinced me that of
all the refugees in the world, of whom I have seen
many, these Tibetans were indeed the most pitiful.

I asked the head of the Indian Red Cross and many others whether additional doctors were needed to help out this situation. They assured me that they were not needed, but that medicines were in short supply, so my appeal to Mr. Thomas was to ask for medical supplies as well as cash. I had promised to call Dr. Dooley and I did to inform him that at this stage doctors and nurses were not needed. He seemed disappointed that he could not render some service at that time, but he assured me of his willingness to do so at any time in the future.

In the spring of 1960 I had to return to America for surgery. I was in the George Washington Hospital in Washington, D.C., when I received a cable from Acharya Kripalani stating that their supply of streptomycin was exhausted, that hundreds of Tibetans were afflicted with t.b. and could I help.

I was a little groggy from my operation which had taken place just 24 hours earlier, but I instinctively took up the phone and called Medico in New York City. I wanted to speak to Dr. Tom Dooley, and fortunately Dr. Dooley was in America for a check-up. I told him that I was calling from the hospital, that we had run out of streptomycin, and that I could not get more until my release from the hospital.

His laugh came over the phone and he said, "So now they are carving on you too. We should get twin beds, in the same hospital!" Then, seriously, he asked: "How much streptomycin do you want, Travis?" When I suggested 2,000 doses, his reply was "Don't be so modest. I will send 3,000 doses by air to India within 24 hours." And so he did.

I returned to the Far East in June and Tom followed

shortly thereafter to resume his work in Laos and begin establishing hospitals in other countries.

My duties in India prevented me from meeting him, but my colleagues and friends in Hong Kong saw to it that Tom was invited to address the Lions Club, the Rotary Club and the American University Club, all of which contributed substantially to his work. By this time he had become as popular in Hong Kong as he was in Laos and elsewhere in the Far East. Through my colleagues Helleck Rose and Bill Howard, who were then representing ARIC, I was able to keep in touch with developments in Hong Kong at that time. When I next saw them several weeks later, they told me that Tom had lost weight but was as enthusiastic and determined as ever.

In September 1960 I received a cable from Tom at my office in New Delhi asking me to come to Bangkok to see him. It so happened that I had scheduled a trip to Hong Kong and on this trip I stopped over to see Tom at his headquarters in the Erawan Hotel in Bangkok. We went up to his room for another of our long talks about refugees and other unfortunate people in Asia and the Far East. His next remark shocked me.

"Travis, I do not know how much longer I will have in which to do the things that are near my heart. Before it is too late I want to make some worthwhile contribution to the unfortunate Tibetan refugees in India. What would you suggest?"

When I recovered from the shock, and saw that he was serious, I said that I doubted whether the Indian government would permit additional foreign agencies to participate in the Tibetan relief program. But I knew of one great need—a mobile clinic to operate in the

187

isolated areas in the foothills of the Himalayan mountains where the roads are only "jeepable," and where medical facilities are scarce. I asked him whether he would care to donate a mobile clinic.

His response was immediate. "Of course I can. Medico will send you two. To whom should the offer be made and how should they be shipped?" I explained that there were many details to be worked out, including free duty entry into India, before the donation should be made, and that these matters could be handled by the Central Relief Committee to which the clinics should be contributed.

"Good, Travis. Explore the possibilities from your end, and I'll get in touch with some people I know up in the Punjab. I shall be in India in November to button up the whole deal."

Thus it was that Tom Dooley, being helpful to others as always, drew me back into close association with him in this final and trying period of his crowded young life.

From New Delhi he flew to Bangkok where he met Dr. H. Leslie Frewing, 53, of Vancouver, Washington, who was to take charge of the hospital in Kuala Lipis, Malaya. Dr. Frewing writes:

We met at the Erawan Hotel and Tom explained that he wanted me to fly first to Muong Sing and Ban Houei Sai in Laos with him and Dr. and Mrs. Bill Van Valin. He explained that weight must be kept minimal, thus no baggage. "Bring a toothbrush and a change of underwear—no more," he said. At breakfast the next morning I was surprised by his attention to detail in that he handed me a flight bag in which to put my scanty gear; a small thoughtfulness but it impressed me.

As I went around Bangkok with Tom for two hours that morning I gained two impressions which persist. He had an excellent technique for getting by the government "front-office boys" by teasing, laughing and joking but always *pushing* until he got into the inner offices where business had to be transacted. Thus he got us visas for Laos although they were not supposed to be issued at that time.

I noticed the great responsibility and dependence Tom imposed on Ted Werner, his pilot. Ted handled the mail, got the plane clearances, bought plane tickets, and even arranged entertainment for the rest of my Malayan team. In those two hours Tom and I were getting visas, I'm sure Ted had to do three times as much work as we did.

The two-hour flight to Vientiane was one of getting acquainted. Pauli Van Valin is an attractive, intelligent, well-informed woman, and she was venturing into the backwoods of Asia for the first time. Bill Van Valin, of course, had been in Laos before, and it was he who had removed the suspicious nodule from Tom's chest the year before. Pauli seemed to be probing Tom's sincerity and motivations. She was a formidable verbal antagonist for him and he seemed puzzled. During the flight Tom made a couple of remarks which might go well only in a very "Bohemian" group. Pauli stopped him coldly, and there were no more such remarks while she was around the next two and one-half days. Tom definitely respected Pauli's type of woman.

We circled over Muong Sing late in the afternoon, and there was pride in Tom's voice as he pointed out "his" hospital. Now, I am one who subscribes to the idea that any good hospital is a matter of teamwork and not a monument to the individual doctor who runs it. So I was a bit taken back by his egotism. When we landed, however, Bill Van Valin said to me, "Now watch his technique." That I did. When the hospital corpsmen arrived Dooley was friendly but he was businesslike. He was obviously in command. He was "Doctor Dooley" to everyone now, and not "Tom." With the local people he was all smiles and pleasant greetings.

The inadequate equipment and "wards" left an immediate and unfavorable impression on me. At times, especially in the Army overseas during World War II, I had been compelled to work with limited equipment and under adverse conditions, but it never had been like this. However, as I watched Tom work and later talked with him, I was satisfied that he was doing his honest best. He was not overstretching his abilities or his equipment. His dedication was entirely practical. He was doing what he could with what he had available, and making no attempt or claim to practicing at Park Avenue medicine or surgery.

That evening I was impressed by the organization and discipline of his hospital and staff. Tom gave orders and they were carried out. His associates seemed to have a hallowed respect for him. He, in turn, had definite pride in his men. He told me: "I have only to say the word and any one of five big medical schools will accept any of these boys." I know that to be true. Three of those men are now in medical school.

Dinner at Muong Sing that evening was indeed an experience. Tom was clad in shirt and sarong. He sat on a high box, padded with pillows, at the head of the table. His staff of six were shaved, bathed, and dressed in clean shirts—which had to be worn neatly tucked inside their jeans. Dinner was roast pork with vegetables and canned fruit—tasty and adequate.

About eleven, Bill and Pauli retired to their platform in one corner of the sleeping room while the rest of us, except Tom, Ron Wintrob and Tom Kirby, lined up on the platform on the other side of the sleeping room which was adjacent to the living-dining area. Tom, Wintrob and Kirby sat up talking until two A.M.

Doctor Wintrob had joined Medico only recently and was to work in Muong Sing. Tom patiently listened to his ideas, then tried to mold Ron's thinking to that which he himself idealized. Over and over he repeated his ideals. His patience seemed infinite, and I knew he must have been tired and sleepy after such a long hard day. Ron harped on a simple matter which seemed to bother him—why couldn't he have a rocking chair flown in? In retrospect that seems foolish, but Tom patiently explained the space aboard the small plane was needed for medicines and other important supplies. Finally they went to bed.

I lay in a sleeping-bag next to Tom. Early the next morning, while he was asleep, I noticed that he was breathing rapidly and shallowly. I thought then that his respiratory capacity was greatly diminished. He must be ill. However, he did not seem short of breath during the day. Never in the week I was with him did he mention or show any evidence of pain—even in the cramped quarters of the plane or while working at Ban Houei Sai.

The only evidence he gave that he knew what fate had in store for him came on our return to Bangkok. I

191

quietly questioned him on a point Marie Ross, one of our nurses, is said to have made, that "Doctor Dooley is full of cancer." Then he told me that he had reason to believe that the malignant melanoma was metastasizing in his blood. If that was true the outcome was inevitable. The only question was: When? There was no further discussion of the matter, and I did not tell our team about it.

The following afternoon we flew over to Ban Houei Sai. Ted made a very hard landing on the short, inadequate airstrip. There was some question of damage to the landing gear. Tom seemed not at all perturbed even though in that remote area damage would have detained us there for perhaps a week. Again he demonstrated his utmost trust in Ted Werner.

Our evening in Ban Houei Sai was much the same as in Muong Sing, but here Tom did not show up so dominantly. He did not know this group so well, they were newer to overseas work. He did show me Terry Cotter's account book, "You should keep one like this in Malaya." But money seemed no great concern to Tom. When he spoke of Medico's specific needs, his usual comment was, "Well, I'll have to give a few more lectures and raise another ten or twelve thousand!"

Tom impressed me in Muong Sing when he generously gave credit to Ron Wintrob for setting up a system of patient records where none had been kept before. Although he had sat up to two A.M. pointing out the errors in Ron's way of doing things, he was as generous in his praise of Ron when he told me of the new record system.

As we flew from Ban Houei Sai to Vientiane, the Van Valins and I got a lesson in how to handle fan mail.

Tom had brought a bundle of perhaps 200 letters from Bangkok, which he opened and read on the plane. He dictated replies on his recorder, set aside one pile of letters for later attention, and another to be handled routinely in New York. His brown leather dispatch case was always at hand and in his spare time he always read and dictated his mail. Thus he lengthened his short days.

On the afternoon of the third day, we landed at Vientiane en route to Bangkok. Ted was ordered to report to Air Control at once. Tom was obviously worried, but he showed his concern only in his clipped speech and the hard look in his eyes. Of course, the surroundings would not inspire confidence in anyone. There were shell holes in the landing strip. The radio in the control tower was dead. No planes were in evidence, and only a few people were around the airport.

Ted hurried to the Air Control Center. He had to walk the half-mile, for there was no transportation available. We waited for nearly an hour and during that time, Captain Kong Le, the rebel paratroop leader, landed in his Dakota and marched past us stiffly without glancing to right or left. Then Ted returned with bad news. He had been refused air clearance. We were stranded in Vientiane.

Tom decided on a desperate gamble. He called Prince Souvanna Phouma on the telephone and explained our predicament. The field was due to close down in ten minutes. The Prince spoke to the Air Control Officer, and in a few short minutes we were on our way south! But not until we were safely within Thailand did we all breathe freely.

Then Tom showed his only evidence of fatigue. Sitting cramped in the back of the plane he grumbled in a frustrated manner, "Why do they do this to me? They know I am only here to help them." He seemed definitely upset that he should be detained. He already had written clearance from both sides in the civil war which was in progress in Laos. That night I had the feeling that Tom Dooley saw the end of Medico in Laos. Even when all were together at dinner I sensed a difference in Tom. He was more reserved and quiet, and definitely worried.

Dr. William B. Van Valin had been in Muong Sing last in July 1959, when he removed surgically from Tom Dooley's chest the "strange black thing" that was later diagnosed as malignant melanoma. Now, in November 1960, he saw a new and different Dooley:

He sat and listened with infinite patience to the boys' problems that had accumulated in his absence. This was a side to Tom that I had not seen, for I had known him as an impulsive, hard-driving young man with a purpose in mind and not a great deal of understanding for those who did not move as fast as he did. Yet here he was in an entirely different role giving advice and expressing views after listening patiently to problems that were present in the minds of the boys.

Watching him, I thought of my earlier visit. Once, after making a trip to the pagoda on the side of the mountain just a stone's throw from Red China, we were journeying homeward when we were met by a Thai Lu man on a small white horse. He had just been to the hospital to get us. His child was having convulsions.

He had a fever for eight days but today was much worse. He asked us to come see the child. After crossing a stream and sloshing through mud that came midway to my knees, we arrived at the stilted house. The child had malaria without a doubt, but he also had "black-water fever" in which the malaria destroys so much blood that it even causes the urine to turn black. The child had severe anemia, and some of the destroyed blood had formed clots in the child's brain causing irreversible convulsions. This is a different type of convulsion from what we know in the States where convulsion is usually associated with temperature. When the temperature drops, the child recovers. But there was no recovery for this child.

The next problem was how to tell the 16-year-old mother that her baby would die shortly. Great sorrow was in her large brown eyes. She was a pretty little thing, and this was her firstborn. Such tragedy is not uncommon in the lives of these people, for every family loses fifty percent of its children at birth or before they are a year old. However, this baby had lived for one year and now was to pass out of the young mother's life. And these people love their children just as much as we love ours.

Later, Tom Dooley explained that the tragedy was even greater in this case. The baby might have had a chance if he had been brought to the doctor sooner. But the child was not brought because this was the rice planting season, and the father and mother could not afford to take time off to walk the miles from their home to the hospital. For these mountain people, a visit to the doctor takes the greater part of a day, and that means a day lost to work in the rice fields. And if the

195

rice is not planted in time the family will starve next
year. There is only a short time during the year when
the upland rice can be planted and that time is precious. So, the child was not brought in and death was
the result.

Tom could hardly blame the father, yet he knew it
was necessary to reprimand him. The father was distraught, but for a different reason. Economically, the
child was important to him. The man who has a large
family is a rich man for he then has insurance for his
old age. The man who has no children starves when he
can no longer work. Such was life in the high valley of
Muong Sing which Tom Dooley had chosen as the setting for his life's work.

I was reminded of another incident which revealed
still another problem Tom had to deal with. One day
we were driving along in the jeep, when Tom came to
a sudden halt, jumped from the jeep and asked me to
follow him. We climbed the ladder to the veranda of a
stilted house, took off our shoes and entered into a dark
room. As my eyes became accustomed to the darkness,
I could see, off in one corner, a woman bent over a pot,
stirring the contents with a stick.

Tom put his pressed hands together in front of his
nose and gave the usual Lao salutation of "*Sambai*,"
but this time he added something to it. He said, "*Sambai Yim Yam*." As he said this, the creature bending
over the pot looked up with a toothless grin and returned the greeting.

I later found out why she was so happy about Tom's
salutation. "*Yim Yam*" means young virgin! Tom was
always a master of flattery, in Asia or America. But here
this flattery had purpose. This toothless hag was the

local witch doctor! This was not all Tom did. He went over, squatted beside the pot, picked up a stick and stirred in the contents with her. She was obviously enjoying every moment of this. It assured her that Tom Dooley was her friend, and that he considered her brand of medicine important in the treatment of the local patients.

Later, Tom told me how Yim Yam helped in many ways. For example, if there was a home that he was unable to get into in order to treat a sick child, he would call Yim Yam. She had great influence in the community and was able to gain entree to homes where Tom could never enter. They would have a consultation. Yim Yam would give the patient some such concoction as the material she was stirring in the pot. Tom would lift the patient's dress and give a shot of penicillin. The patient would get well and give Yim Yam two coconuts, one of which she would give to Tom. On other occasions, Yim Yam would not be getting the desired response from some patient she was treating. She would call in Tom for a consultation, and he would take over. The patient would get well and Tom would be paid the two coconuts. He in turn would give one to Yim Yam.

To me this exemplified Tom Dooley's deep understanding of the people he was dealing with and the extent to which he would go in order to help them. Many people have thought that Tom Dooley introduced the witch doctors into his books and lectures merely for their oddity and humor. The witch doctors were indeed a very real problem. They could have defeated all Dooley was trying to do in Muong Sing. They could have been implacable enemies and done great harm;

instead he made them his friends and thus was able to control them.

*November 13-21.* Copenhaver and Malcolm Dooley arrived in Bangkok on November 13. Dr. Edgar F. Berman, President of Medico, and his wife were already there for a brief visit on their way from Japan to Africa where Dr. Berman planned to spend six weeks in Albert Schweitzer's hospital in Lambarene. The next morning the whirlwind inspection began with a trip to Cambodia; in thirteen days Bob and Malcolm covered all Medico installations in Cambodia, Laos and Vietnam.

Bob Copenhaver's report gives a close-up view of Dooley operating in the field at that time:

When we arrived I was not aware of any change in Tom's physical condition. He looked well enough, showed his usual inexhaustable energy and seemed in good spirits. He had a lot on his mind, obviously, for in addition to all his routine worries he had the Bermans and us to take care of, and the abortive revolt against Ngo Dinh Diem had just occurred in Vietnam —as a matter of fact we saw the rebel generals and colonels arrive in Cambodia seeking asylum when we landed in Phnom Penh. But I would say Tom was taking everything in his stride.

We were delayed in Phnom Penh for a couple of days because of mechanical trouble with the plane, and Dr. and Mrs. Berman returned to Bangkok by commercial airline. The impatient, irritable Tom was suddenly back with us. Malcolm and I were having a cool glass of Cambodian beer in the hotel café. Tom came and sat down with us. We said we were going to eat dinner right there. "Oh, no," said Tom, "We'll go out to the home of an old friend of mine. But first I'm going up to lie down."

Three hours later Tom still hadn't shown up. We went to his room and had great difficulty awakening him. He was out cold. We got no explanation then or later, and I can only assume that he had been in pain or had taken something to make him sleep. For the remaining ten or twelve days we were with him, he went slowly but steadily downhill.

Ted Werner asked us to talk to Tom about slowing down. Ted said, "He won't listen to me, but he has great respect for you. Do something about it, because he's killing himself." I tried to talk to Tom, but all I got was an angry brush-off. Nothing could stop him now in his headlong drive to get things done. This caused Malcolm and me to reflect on his remark in October about not being here after January 1st. We both had related that to his desire to return to New York to run Medico. However, we now agreed that Tom had known even then that his time was short. Perhaps I can say that I was convinced that Tom was going to die, but I couldn't say when or how soon. It looked as though the guy could collapse at any minute.

With the Medico plane still out of commission, Tom prevailed upon a wonderful young American girl, the wife of the agricultural attaché, to fly us to Kratie and Ratanakiri in an old Cessna borrowed from the Cambodian Air Force. She was a licensed pilot and was eager to get in as much flying time as possible in order

199

to maintain proficiency. We spent a couple of days there and then went over to Viet Nam by commercial airline.

Tom was concerned about the political situation in Saigon but only as it effected his new hospital up in Quang Ngai and the An-Lac Orphanage. He was eager to have us meet Madame Ngai and, of course, he never went to Saigon without paying a visit there. Frankly, I had heard so much about the An-Lac Orphanage that I expected to be disappointed by the place as a reality. On the contrary, I was pleasantly surprised, even over-whelmed, by its adequacy. And Tom's spirits picked up amazingly as soon as we arrived there—he seemed to be the old energetic, high-spirited Tom Dooley again.

They had set about a dozen old Quonset huts and prefabricated Navy warehouse buildings within a com-pound, and these were well furnished and arranged efficiently. There must have been about 400 children living there at that time, and about 90 or 100 were less than a year old. The nursery, in fact, was a bit over-crowded. There would be a hammock strung between every two cribs. I was told that a new baby is found on the An-Lac doorstep every two or three days.

Madame Ngai runs the whole show herself with the help of three old women and several of the teen-age orphans. But, of course, all the kids work, the older ones taking care of the small children and babies. Everybody takes care of everybody else—that, I think, is largely responsible for the wonderfully happy spirit of the place, which is otherwise undefinable. Many of the original orphans—the An-Lac "alumni"—are now working as clerks, waiters, busboys, and airline stew-ards, but they all come back on Saturdays and Sundays, the girls to help Madame Ngai with the children and the household chores, and the men to do all sorts of carpentry and maintenance jobs. An-Lac is truly an inspiring place.

Madame Ngai, who is every bit as wonderful and charming as Dooley described her, had a dinner party for us that evening that would have made Pearl Mesta green with envy. The other guests were generals, admirals, diplomats, the Minister of Health and several other cabinet officers. The food and wines were excellent, although a bit on the exotic side. But it was a thrill to see Tom eat something for a change. He had no appetite, and always lost what little he ate.

We left Madame Ngai's house quite late that evening, but Tom's happy mood prevailed until we reached the hotel. "Wasn't that wonderful?" he kept asking. "Isn't it even more than you expected?"

In the hotel lobby, he handed Malcolm some local currency and said, "You fellows go somewhere and have a beer. I'm going to bed." He was gone before we could say a word. We could only speculate on what was wrong. Probably he was ill from the food he had eaten, and didn't want to destroy the bright illusions he had created for us that evening.

The next day we flew in a government plane to Tourane where Tom was sure the Minister of Health of the province would furnish a jeep to take us to Quang Ngai. At the Tourane airport he telephoned and a jeep was sent to bring us into the town. But when Tom asked for a driver to take us to Quang Ngai we were turned down cold.

"You can't go to Quang Ngai."

"Why?"

"There's a curfew."

"We're going anyway."

"You can't. The Communists will shoot you. It's too late to send a wireless that you're coming through."

In the end, of course, Tom Dooley prevailed. We left at 5:10 P.M., and the worried little Vietnamese who had been ordered to drive us kept glancing at the setting sun while driving at 80 mph over the 120 miles of rough roads. We didn't pass a single vehicle on the way.

What Malcolm and I hadn't realized was that the Province of Quang Ngai (population about 700,000) is just near enough to the border to be about half Communist and half non-Communist. This is not to say that many people are confirmed or believing Communists; they just consider it safer to declare or pretend a Communist allegiance. There is a great deal of Communist guerrilla warfare and terrorism in this part of the Republic, and consequently the Quang Ngai hospital was already getting its share of atrocity cases. For example, an old man would be found on the road with one leg completely crushed by heavy stones. Tied around his neck would be a sign: "Join the Communists, and this won't happen to you." The Medico hospital was averaging 15 or 20 such cases per day and I believe they once had 70 atrocity cases in one night.

We arrived at Quang Ngai at about 8:30 that night. Dr. Wiedermann informed us that we had to go to the dinner given by the governor of the province. That was the time Malcolm and I unwittingly savored a dish of dog and pigeon; we didn't become ill until later when we found out what it was.

One of the Vietnamese male nurses at the hospital, who was assigned to me as guide and interpreter, was a Communist. No one seemed to think anything of it. He was the only trained nurse available, and he worked just as hard to save non-Communist lives.

I found him extremely intelligent, and he seemed interested in learning the American way of life. He asked me if I would be his sponsor so he could come to the United States. But he said he also wanted to go to Moscow. Why was he a Communist? Simply because he had come from the North, and if you were not a Communist in North Vietnam you did not eat and you probably wouldn't live. This fellow simply couldn't see the point in being a dead pro-Westerner so, in effect, he was keeping his Communist "life insurance" in full force and effect.

Communist atrocities were old stuff to Tom Dooley, and he has seen things far worse than what was going on in Quang Ngai. But Malcolm and I found some of the tales hair-raising. For example, the public school system is very good in South Vietnam. In Quang Ngai province, where the terrorism is most vicious, the school buses are stopped frequently. A Communist spokesman will get aboard the bus and announce: "I represent the Viet Minh. We will cut off the right hand of everybody who is on this bus tomorrow afternoon."

When the bus comes by the next afternoon, there are soldiers aboard as guards, so nothing happens. But maybe two weeks later, when they finally drop the guard, the same fellow will appear. He stops the bus, gets on board, and cuts off the first joint of a child's finger. Then he says: "We will cut off the rest of that finger tomorrow—and the next day the entire hand."

You can imagine the effect this has on parents. When

no children show up, the bus stops running, and school closes. That is exactly what the Communists want.

Quang Ngai province, with its miles of beautiful sand beach, could be the Riviera of the Far East. Tourane and Hue, nearer the 17th parallel, were built by the French as resort towns, and people came there from Saigon and other inland cities for their holidays. But now no one goes to Quang Ngai who doesn't have to. Terrorism was so bad that the army was shifting all men to civilian clothes. It was so funny to see them walking along the streets trying to conceal their sub-machine guns under their coats or in their trousers.

We stayed in Quang Ngai only one night, then we returned to Saigon and from there we went to Vientiane via airline.

*November 22-25.* When we arrived in Vientiane we were already a day or two behind schedule because of loss of the Piper Apache. Tom was crestfallen. He felt we'd never see Muong Sing because we couldn't commandeer an airplane in Vientiane. Then, suddenly, while we were sitting in front of the hotel, we looked up and saw the Piper Apache circling over Vientiane. As soon as it landed, we loaded up everything and took off for Muong Sing.

The Muong Sing hospital was in excellent condition. Dr. Wintrob was in charge, and Tom Kirby, Alan Rommel, and John Kim were the corpsmen. They had another bear-mauling case. Tom laughed and said: "*Life* magazine says that everytime I have a visitor in Muong Sing I trot out my case of bear-mauling. They don't know that it's a different case every time."

This case was a little old fellow who had had his nose

mauled by a bear. The boys called him "No-Nose Ma-goo." They were keeping the wound from becoming infected while they waited a surgeon. Tom told Dr. Wintrob how to do the operation.

Late that afternoon we flew over to Ban Houei Sai, an incredibly beautiful place. You stand on a river bed at the end of nowhere and look up at snow-capped mountains, and down upon a green plain of rice-pad-dies that stretches clear to the rugged mountains of Laos and Red China. You can see four different coun-tries—Laos, Thailand, Red China and Burma—all from this one vantage point.

We drove by jeep into the village for the wedding of the daughter of the mayor. She was marrying the local agent for Air Laos, a pretty easy job in Ban Houei Sai because they only have two flights a week by one single-engine aircraft. When the mayor heard Dooley was in town the doctor had to join in the marriage feast. They gave each of us a water-glass full of liquor to toast the bride. It's 170 proof and you're supposed to drink it in one gulp. That one glass is enough to make you com-pletely drunk.

We returned to the house and talked until about 3:00 A.M. Tom scheduled two operations for the morn-ing. He went down first to check on sick call and ex-amine a couple of questionable cases Estelle Hughes had called in as soon as Dr. Dooley arrived. Sick call was unusually large that morning because the women had brought their children in from the hinterlands the day before when they saw the little blue airplane fly over the village.

Then Tom went ahead with his scheduled operations. There was a Black Thai girl who had a bad cleft lip

205

which had become infected. Ordinarily, this would have been elective surgery but, because of this infection, it had become a matter of life or death. Tom got a book down from the shelf, and reviewed exactly what had to be done with Dr. Hughes and little Jan Cotter, the nurse. Then he took a sheet of paper and drew what the lip should look like after surgery. They took calipers and measured the area to be incised and marked the places where sutures were to be placed, etc.

There is a superstition among the Black Thai tribe that children must never cry. If a child cries it is possessed by a devil and the child will die. Tom showed the Black Thai mother pictures of another Black Thai girl before and after a similar operation and assured her that even though her child cried a bit the operation would be safe and successful. It must have taken him about an hour to prepare for the operation.

This was the first time I had seen "his" operating room. It was fantastic. The table was made of wood, but it was made so it could be raised or lowered to any height by a system of pegs. The light shade was also made of wood lined with aluminum foil for reflective quality. The light itself was powered by a gasoline-driven generator which wasn't started until the very last second so as not to waste gasoline which, of course, had to be flown in and was in short supply because of the war.

Tom gave the girl a mild anesthetic, not strong enough to knock her out, but sufficient to mask the pain. He was trying to keep her at a stage where her gag reflex would work so that she wouldn't swallow blood. The worried mother stood just outside the door with her nose pressed against the screen for the next two hours. Inevitably, the child sobbed and cried and the mother became hysterical. Tom said: "Damn it, get the ether!"

Estelle Hughes had been called out of the operating room to handle some sort of emergency. So I had to administer the ether while Dr. Tom finished the long and delicate operation with only Jan Cotter's assistance. I'm happy to say that the outcome was an immense success.

I'm sure Tom was having a lot of pain at this time. But he did a magnificent job of concealing it. He was taking no drugs because he wanted a clear mind and a steady hand when doing surgery. He made the ward rounds with Jan Cotter. Jan explained each case, what the medication had been thus far, what the surgical procedure had been, what they planned to do, etc. Tom agreed with what they were doing in all but one case, and he didn't discuss that with Jan Cotter but later discussed the case with Dr. Hughes.

Then we got in the airplane, flew to Vientiane, and on to Bangkok. Malcolm was sitting in front next to Ted Werner, and Tom and I were sitting together in the rear. There was the beautiful Asian sunset, which seemed to be directly under us. Suddenly a small thundercloud, completely black, came along and blotted out the sun, although you could still see the brilliance of the sun's rays above and beyond.

Tom said, "That's my life. The horizon is unlimited. There is nothing that can stop me—except a black cloud of melanoma." In ten seconds the wind blew the cloud away and again we saw the beauty of the sunset. "See, Tom, how quickly it passes!" I said.

Tom said, "My black cloud will never pass."

207

The next morning (November 26) in Bangkok Tom did the Christmas tape which was distributed as a record to a number of people. Then, before we left for Hong Kong, he packed everything so that he need not worry about coming back. Tom always kept a couple of sea chests or footlockers at the hotel into which he threw everything he didn't need. He would close them up, give the bellboy 50 cents, and say, "Store them." This time he didn't do that.

He folded everything very neatly. He put a lot of his papers in a big stamped envelope and gave it to Ted and said, "I may ask you to mail these to me." When we took off for Hong Kong I felt that Tom had decided to fly back to the States—to stay.

When I left Tom at the airport in Hong Kong it was typical of every time I ever left him. There were no goodbyes. He just said: "So long, Bob. Take care of yourself. I'll run ahead and make sure you get a good seat on the jet all the way back to San Francisco." That was it. No shaking of hands. I went downstairs, talked to the ticket agent, and then walked across the compound. Tom came back, and said, "I didn't say good-bye to you right."

I said, "It's just like the Waldorf. You take an elevator going up, and I get on one going down. We never get to say hello or goodbye."

"But I want to say goodbye this time," he said. "I'm sure glad you got to see Laos before anything happened."

He reached over the corrugated steel barrier and shook my hand. As I pulled it back I cut my arm, and the blood came through the sports shirt I was wearing. Tom looked at it and said, "Well, you have something

208

to remember Asia by." Then he turned around and walked down the alley between the two buildings. I watched him go—limping on his one bad leg.

Shortly after Bob Copenhaver's departure, the phone rang in Travis Fletcher's room. It was Tom Dooley.

"Travis, I don't think I can make it back to Laos as I planned. Who is your doctor? What hospital were you in? That's where I ought to go for a rest, at least. I'm completely exhausted."

Two hours later, he was a patient in St. Theresa's Hospital, occupying the same big room Fletcher had vacated only three weeks earlier.

"Later in the evening Tom called me again," Travis Fletcher reports. "He was lonesome, and he was also hungry for 'some real good Chinese food.' I had two full-course Chinese dinners delivered to his room, and I sat there talking to him for several hours while he merely picked at the food.

"He asked me to do what I could to keep his presence in the hospital from getting into the press—that would only worry his mother and make a big splash in the American newspapers. He promised to telephone his mother in the morning—'after they make some X-rays; that's the most important thing.'

"The next day, when I saw him again in the hospital, he showed me the X-ray films, and pointed to some white spots along the spinal column. 'That's why I'm in such pain,' he told me. 'Travis, this thing has gone into my spine. Good God, and I still have so much work to do!"

*December 5-8.* Gerry Gerold stopped over in Hong Kong on December 5, en route from his headquarters in Delhi to the United States. Jerry O'Donnell, Hong Kong area director for Pan Am, told him Dooley was in St. Theresa's Hospital, reportedly in bad shape. Gerold arrived just as Tom Dooley was being discharged. Gerry Gerold says:

In four weeks a complete change had taken place. I was shocked to see Tom so thin and pale, practically bent when standing, and obviously suffering terrific pain in his back. The poor guy found it difficult to lower himself into a chair, and even more difficult to get out of it and on his feet.

We had a long talk concerning his condition and he told me quite confidentially that he felt almost certain the old trouble had returned. He had talked to his New York doctors on the telephone and was then awaiting their diagnosis. But Tom had only one thing on his mind—to do as much as he could in the short time he had, for he knew then that his days were numbered.

I tried to persuade Tom to go to New York immediately but he said that was impossible because he still had so many things to do in Vietnam, Cambodia and Laos before leaving for New York in January to attend the Medico Board meeting. Anyone who knew Tom will agree, I'm sure, there was no changing the Dooley mind mind once it was made up.

210

During the next few days, while we were awaiting our respective planes—he going to Bangkok and I to Honolulu—we managed to have a pleasant time in Hong Kong, despite Tom's painful condition. We had a grand reunion with Bill Quinn, the governor of our newest state, Hawaii, and his lovely wife, Nancy, both of whom hail from St. Louis, Missouri. It was then that Tom started to refer jokingly to his spinal pain as 'me and my aching back'! How he remained so cheerful, jovial, and seemingly happy, I'll never understand. Here was a dying man, with an air of bravado and a will-to-do, and he never uttered a complaint. The only complaints we heard from Tom were directed at those people who had not been very generous to his appeals, and who, in his opinion could have well afforded an occasional donation. But he wasn't bitter—Tom just wanted more money for his hospitals!

On my last evening in Hong Kong, Tom and I were invited to have a family dinner with Jerry O'Donnell and his gracious wife, Susan, and their three children. It was a memorable and sad evening. We all knew that Tom could not live many more months, and yet we all carried on as though we had not a care in the world. He spent most of the time with the O'Donnell children, reading to the little boy, or coddling the small baby, a recent addition to the O'Donnell clan. Tom talked about the brace which had not yet arrived from the States, and jokingly begged Susan to lend him the brace she had discarded after a recent bout with a slipped disc. Much to Susan's embarrassment, he held it up for all to see and called it "Susan's Corset." (The brace did arrive the next day but I don't think it helped Tom's aching back.)

That was our last evening together. On our way back to the Kowloon Side, the mainland, where our hotel was located, Tom suggested that instead of taking the usual ferry boat which makes the trip between Hong Kong and Kowloon in a matter of minutes, we take the slower but more typical sampan, or small Chinese junk. At the moment, I couldn't understand why Tom, tired as he was, wanted a "slow boat to China." But once we were under way, he kept his eyes fixed on the magnificent sight of Hong Kong at night. I suddenly understood. Tom was seeing one of his favorite sights for the last time.

Next day, before my departure, we met for lunch and decided to make a celebration of it. I'm sure the Peninsular Hotel never served a stranger luncheon—old fashioneds and caviar! I remember asking Tom jokingly during that luncheon if he had kept his promise to say the first Rosary for me when he used the Pope John XXIII beads I had given him in Delhi. His reply was typically Tom Dooley: "Listen, Bub, I need all the prayers I can get, including my own. So you take care of your own beads!"

Tom was a real operator, and he knew it! He had a way of making people feel that they couldn't do enough for him, not that he needed anything for himself. During that last luncheon I was wearing an unusual Swiss watch, which had been given to me by my good friend Jules Stein, president of Music Corporation of America. It had a tiny light bulb on the dial which illuminated the face at the press of a small button, and the light was powered by a tiny battery inside the case. Tom was like a small child seeing a new toy. He said, seriously: "You know, with a watch like that I could tell

212

the hour in the jungle at any time of night!" Of course, I gave Tom the watch—and I'm sure Jules Stein won't mind.

When the time came for me to leave for the airport, I saw Tom struggling along through the lobby. His movements were very labored and obviously painful. I pounced upon him with a "Where in hell do you think you are going?" And he said, "To the airport to see you off! People are always seeing me off—so it's time I made an effort for someone else!" Tom saw me off at Hong Kong airport. My last sight of him was just a glimpse from the window as our giant 707 Clipper zoomed down the runway.

*December 8-9.* The brace, made in Florida and flown to Hong Kong by Pan American, arrived late on the afternoon of December 8. Strapping it on and wearing it was torture, but Tom Dooley knew it was necessary to support his disintegrating vertebrae, and he hoped it might relieve pressure on the nerves. So he wore and endured it, and thereafter referred to it as the "Iron Maiden."

Then he called Ted Werner in Bangkok and ordered him to fly up to Muong Sing and pick up Dr. Alex Zlatanos, the new Kratie surgeon who was on temporary duty in Laos. "I'll take a commercial plane to Bangkok and meet both of you there tomorrow." Dooley said. "I want to have a talk with Alex before he returns to Kratie."

The next evening (December 9) Ted Werner and

Dr. Zlatanos were waiting at the Bangkok airport when Dooley's plane arrived.

Alexandros Zlatanos, 32 years old, was a dark-eyed, swarthy, "Rock of Gibralter" type of man who had received his medical degree from the University of Thessaloniki, Greece, in 1955. He then came to America, served his internship in a Chicago hospital, and completed his residency in general surgery at the Reading Hospital, Reading, Pennsylvania. Shortly before he completed his resident's training, he heard that Medico needed surgeons and volunteered to serve in Southeast Asia. Says Zlatanos:

I met Dr. Tom Dooley in October 1960, when he returned to New York for his medical checkup. He had arrived early that same day after flying halfway around the world. Any other sick man who had made such a tiring journey would have been in bed resting. I found Tom looking for some papers in a file cabinet in the Medico office.

"Tom, I want you to meet Alex Zlatanos who is going to Cambodia for us," his brother Malcolm said when we entered the office. Tom Dooley gave me a warm smile, and put out his left hand for me to shake.

"Welcome aboard, Alex! Sit down. I want to talk to you." Immediately I felt as though I had known him for years.

Because his schedule was so tight, he asked me to go with him to the office of a radiologist where he had his chest X-rayed. During the next two hours, Tom Dooley talked and I listened. He told me about his work, and about the hardships and rewards of a Medico doctor.

214

His voice was full of compassion when he talked about the people I would soon be serving in Southeast Asia.

As he went on describing the future of Medico, I wondered: How can any man speak so confidently of the future when he knows his days are so short? We all live under a sentence of death, but this man knows that his death warrant is already signed.

Driving back to Reading, Pennsylvania, where I had much to do before my departure for Cambodia, I tried to sort out my impressions of Tom Dooley. He had a strong personality, boundless energy, real courage, and a deep compassion for suffering mankind. But he didn't strike me at all like the Dr. Tom Dooley, popular hero and crusading missionary, I had read about in the newspapers. Missionaries invariably operate in a limited area; Tom Dooley wanted to reach out and help every wretched human being on earth. Heroes are usually confronted by inescapable circumstances and choose to fight instead of to run; Tom Dooley had gone out seeking the circumstances, and then had started his own struggle against them. No, I decided, Tom Dooley was something more than a missionary or a conventional hero. He was an honest human being of a high order. He was a physician who accepted conscientiously the highest responsibilities of his profession and was trying honestly to fulfill them. He was a fine man, and I would be happy and honored to serve under him.

The next time I saw Tom was a month later, in November, on the narrow, grass-covered airstrip at Kratie, Cambodia. His condition had deteriorated noticeably within that month, yet he seemed to have greater drive. He stayed at Kratie only a short time, but he inspected everything, checked over our patients, talked

215

to everyone on the staff individually, and solved a lot of problems and made firm decisions. He reminded me of a father taking care of the family's needs before leaving on a long trip.

Before he took off in the Apache, he called me aside. "Alex, everything seems in pretty good shape here," he said. "In the next couple of weeks I want you to fly up to Laos and take care of the surgical cases in Muong Sing and Ban Houei Sai. Make arrangements with Ted about the airplane."

And that was how I happened to be waiting for him at the Bangkok Airport on his evening of December 9. I had completed my assignment in Laos, and now I was asking myself if it had really been worthwhile. I had performed three operations in Muong Sing and only one in Ban Houei Sai. Had I remained in Kratie, I could have easily accomplished three times as much work. Why had Tom sent me to Laos? Within a few minutes after his airplane landed I had the answer.

Tom got off the plane from Hong Kong slowly. The cancer was spreading fast in his back and right shoulder, and the "Iron Maiden" obviously restricted his movements. But he didn't want to talk about himself. The first thing he asked me was how the operation on the woman with the hole in her cheek had turned out!

This woman had been an old patient of Tom's in Muong Sing. A long neglected abscess in her jaw had finally made a gaping hole in her left cheek. The infection and scar tissue had so constricted her face that she was barely able to open her mouth, so she found it easier to shovel the rice through the hole. Despite this "convenience," she was ashamed of that hole in her face and had begged Tom to do something about it.

216

Another visiting surgeon had done a "tube flap" graft to the left side of her face and it had been my job to perform the second stage of the operation and close the defect. When I told him that the surgery had been successful Tom heaved a great sigh of relief and thanked me profusely. "Thank God," he exclaimed. "You know, I promised that poor woman that we would do something for her. And now we've done it. I don't know how to thank you, Alex."

Then I knew why I was sent to Laos. To Tom Dooley, "Promises to keep" was more than a line in a poem by Robert Frost. It was part of his life.

He had a huge amount of stuff to clear through customs, but I noticed that only a small suitcase and a typewriter were his personal belongings. The rest consisted of surgical instruments, pharmaceuticals, and Christmas gifts for all the members of the Medico teams in Laos, Vietnam, Malaya, and Cambodia. Later, in his hotel room, I helped him sort out the gifts to be sent to the various teams because he could not use his right arm. He was uncomfortable in the brace so he took it off, but immediately the pain became worse. He showed me the X-rays of his spine with the unmistakable signs of bone destruction. When I saw those shadows on the film, my heart sank. The question was: How much longer?

Despite his condition, he kept on talking about his plans to visit the other teams, to spend Christmas in Muong Sing, and to return to the States for another coast-to-coast fund-raising tour. Then I saw his overwhelming sadness, and I knew that his real agony came not primarily from his physical condition but from an awareness that his physical condition would never permit him to do all the things he had to do.

I saw him once more when he spent a day (December 16) at Kratie a week later. The pain was getting more severe by the day. He ate almost nothing, and was taking codeine or demerol every few hours. Physically he was breaking down fast, but he was driving himself almost desperately. But he still wouldn't talk about himself, and seemed obsessed with even the most minor problems of the Kratie hospital. He told me that I should order screens for the entire house, and cut down the abundant tropical vegetation that was inundating the place. I could not understand how any man in such excruciating pain, knowing he is dying, could give a damn about unscreened windows and uncut foliage.

Dr. Rosenbloom's wife, Edith, was due to have her baby that day, and Tom wanted to remain and assist in the delivery. But his time was running short, and the Piper Apache came to pick him up while we still had Edith Rosenbloom in the operating room. The last I saw of him was when he peeked into the room and waved goodbye to us. When I looked up at him he frowned and shook his head and pointed to the draped figure on the table as if to say: "Doctor, remember who you are and the high duty you are about to perform."

There was a momentary silence in the Kratie operating room as Tom Dooley walked out of our lives forever. But in that same moment the silence was broken by a loud wail, and Arlen Rosenbloom's son was born, reminding all of us of the Divine Wisdom of life and death.

*December 10-13.* Ted Werner induced Dooley to fly from Bangkok to Saigon by a commercial airliner, while he flew Alex Zlatanos to Kratie in the Piper Apache. "I promised to join him in Saigon the following morning," Ted says. "I was convinced that Tom's days of flying in the 'pigeon-hole' of the Piper Apache were about over, although I knew he probably wouldn't agree. However, he knew that it was important for Dr. Zlatanos to get back to his job in Kratie so he consented to the arrangement."

Dooley arrived in Saigon on December 10th and went directly to the Majestic Hotel. This time there was no visit to the An-Lac Orphanage. Tom Dooley was much too sick, so Madame Ngai came to visit him in the hotel on the evening of December 11th.

Madame Ngai recalls:

He was in very low spirits. I had never seen Tom Dooley really depressed before. For a little while I tried to laugh and joke as we did in the old days. But Tom didn't respond and my heart wasn't in it anyway. He admitted to me, for the first time, that he knew his hours were numbered. He kept saying, "But somehow I must go on. I simply *must*. I must go up to Quang Ngai tomorrow. Then I must fly up to Muong Sing and Ban Houei Sai and get things settled there. The hardest part of it is going to be to conceal the condition I am in." There were real tears streaming down his face. He said: "The others must never see me like this. It would destroy everything."

This was more than I could bear, so we both cried a great deal that evening. Even then, Tom tried to console me and to lift my spirits. "You have had a wonder-

219

ful life," he told me, "And you still have a wonderful life before you. But you must never stop fighting. Keep up your faith. Pray and work, and put all your energy into the great task God has given to you. You will never fail."

Ted Werner returned late that evening, and peeked into Tom's room. When he saw the tearful scene with Madame Ngai, he quietly closed the door and went away. Next morning, obedient to Tom's orders, he had the airplane ready for the flight to Quang Ngai. But someone had forgotten to obtain an authorization for the flight, and they were forced to wait while Madame Ngai employed her considerable influence and charm to obtain the necessary papers from the bureaucrats. Then they took off Tuesday morning and flew toward Quang Ngai.

Dooley was still in low spirits. "Tom, I really think you ought to buck up or else abandon this trip," Ted Werner said. "The Quang Ngai team simply must not see you as I saw you last night when I got back to the hotel. You will simply crush their spirits, and defeat the purpose of this trip. Either snap out of it, or let's go home."

"Don't worry!" Dooley assured him. "I won't let them down. I guess I've just reached a point where I can no longer hide things from a few people like you and Madame Ngai. But I can still put on a pretty good act for the others. Just wait and see."

*December 13.* Ted saw the dramatic change in Dooley almost as the plane touched down in Quang Ngai. Dr. Wiedermann and Al Harris were pleasantly surprised when Tom crawled out of the plane, awkwardly and painfully, but still smiling—the same old Tom Dooley.

"I knew that he had been in the hospital while he was in Hong Kong and I had heard that there was a suspected metastasis of the cancer to his spine," Wiedermann says. "So I really didn't expect him to come to Quang Ngai, and was surprised when the Apache flew over, then touched down at the airport and out stepped Dr. Dooley wearing the brace. Of course, he had lost a terrific amount of weight, and he was pale and haggard, but he seemed bursting with energy. He talked with me for hours and hours until late that night.

"He outlined all the things he had done in Hong Kong, told me all the things he had bought. He did mention his admission to the hospital and the pain he was having in the back of his spine, but he treated it lightly. He did say that he was going back to the States soon for a medical check-up. But told me over and over again that he would be back in Quang Ngai by March. He was so convincing that I was sure he would be with us then.

Ted Werner was amazed and then worried when the talk went on late into the night. Dr. Wiedermann finally excused himself, saying that he was dead tired, and went to bed. Tom made no move to quit, but sat up discussing staff and supply problems with Al Harris, the young ex-Navy corpsman from Hagerstown, Maryland. Only after Al begged that the hour was late and he had early duties in the morning, did Dooley give up. Before he went to bed, he drew Ted Werner aside.

"How did I do?" he asked. "Do you think I let them down?"

"Tom, you gave an amazing performance! I swear, I've never witnessed anything like it!"

Ted Werner, recalling that night, says: "And I meant every word I said. He was absolutely amazing. Many months later, Carl Wiedermann, who is a very perceptive physician, told me that Tom Dooley had actually convinced him that night that he was on the mend."

*December 14.* Dooley, Werner and Dr. Carl Wiedermann left together in the morning and flew down to Saigon. Dr. Wiedermann recalls:

That whole day he followed me from one office to another, straightening out all our bureaucratic troubles with the government. He was wearing the brace and constantly kidding about it. When different officials asked him about his health he would always say: "Oh, it's not so bad. I don't think my last hour has yet come." He would always laugh and smile about it.

It was a *very* hot and a *very* tiresome day. He told me, "Carl, you're doing a fine job at Quang Ngai."

I had sudden misgivings about that, and unthinkingly said something to the effect that there was *still so much to do*.

He laughed and reminded me again of the two ways of describing a cup of tea: one is to say that the cup is half empty; the other, to say that the cup is half full. "You always say it is half empty, Carl. Why can't you say it's half full? Why don't you see what you have achieved so far, and be thankful that you have plenty of time to achieve more?"

Before they left Saigon for Phnom Penh, Cambodia, Tom insisted that he wanted to visit the sidewalk café of the Continental Palace Hotel, which held many memories of the old days. Reluctantly, Ted Werner agreed to go along, reminding Tom that it would be better if he got some rest.

"No, we'll sit outside the Continental and have some food and a drink," Tom Dooley said. "I remember how I used to sit there in the old days and watch the Vietnamese girls ride by on their bicycles with their dresses flowing in the breeze. I'd just like to know if it is still the same."

Ted Werner wanted to take a cab, but Dooley insisted upon walking.

"As we were walking down Catinat Street," Ted Werner recalls, "we saw an elderly Vietnamese walking along pushing a brand new bicycle, with two young children tagging along behind him. When the old man saw Dooley he stopped and said, '*Bon soir, Monsieur le Docteur!*'

223

"Golly! This was the best medicine Tom had had in many a month. His face lighted up, and they began an animated conversation in French. Afterwards Tom told me that the old fellow was one of the refugees he had helped evacuate from Haiphong in 1955."

When they got to the Continental, Tom Dooley would not eat or drink a thing. He told Ted that the place was entirely different. "The old spirit's gone," he said. The street was too crowded, the bicycles looked too new, and he grumbled that "I'll bet all those darn dresses bear labels, 'Made in America.'"

Madame Ngai joined them, and she urged Tom to eat something. He jokingly told her that the only thing that appealed to his appetite was stuffed celery—knowing quite well that celery was a luxury and was not grown anywhere in Southeast Asia.

"However," says Ted Werner, "Dooley for once had forgotten about Madame Ngai and her influential connections. When we left our hotel for the airport the next morning, a couple of the An-Lac orphans were waiting for us in the lobby with a covered tray. When they removed the napkin, there we saw our stuffed celery! Madame Ngai had apparently telephoned some of her friends, and they had obtained it from the commissary. The children at the orphanage had stuffed about half the celery stalks with cream cheese. They handed us the rest of the stalks plus the jar of cheese and a knife so that we could finish it on the plane going to Phnom Penh."

They piled their baggage into a car, and Madame Ngai and the two children accompanied them to the airport. Dooley and Ted sat in the front seat with the driver, while Madame Ngai and the children sat in the rear. "On the way," says Ted, "Dooley nibbled on the celery moodily. Then he gave me a startled look, and kept poking me in the ribs. I couldn't figure out what it was all about. Finally, while Madame Ngai and the children were chattering loudly in French, Tom whispered to me: 'There's broken glass in that cheese! The kids must have dropped the jar! Don't eat it!'

"We stowed the plate of stuffed celery and the jar of cheese in the cockpit of the plane, and said goodbye to Madame Ngai and the kids. The odor of the cheese in the hot cockpit served to keep us awake, at least. We weren't able to dump the stuff until we landed in Phnom Penh."


*December 15.* They checked in at Phnom Penh, and Dooley immediately wanted to see the McCarthys. He had brought a record for John McCarthy, and on the way he insisted upon buying some roses for Pat.

Pat McCarthy writes:

We knew that the days were running out for Tom, but the news from Hong Kong had been a staggering blow. We were sure that he would go right back to the States. But on the 15th of December, the doorbell rang

225

and we found him on our doorstep, clutching a big bunch of roses for me and a record for John. He and Ted Werner had just arrived from Saigon where he had gone to say goodbye to Madame Ngai. He was wearing his "Iron Maiden." My heart began to crack that day. For the next four days I think we all died a little.

The title of the record he brought for John was "Music for Reading" to which he had added, "Tom Dooley's latest book by." Among the selections on the disc was Clair de Lune, which he loved. He wanted music playing all the time he was here.

For the next few days he and Ted stayed at the hotel, but Tom came to our apartment regularly for hot showers. Heat seemed to help a bit. We were frantic at being so helpless. Our little Vietnamese maid was in tears because he would not eat! For days he hadn't eaten anything but fruit and soup. He said he thought maybe he could eat a steak and french fries, so we had that for him on Saturday night. He ate one bite of meat and one potato, and went back to the couch. Ted, Wayne McKinney, Clint Chambers, John and I finished, while he lay on the couch, nibbling at some Christmas hard candy and talking about Medico.

Later, some of our friends dropped in to meet him. He was sitting, Indian fashion, on the couch, wearing John's blue corduroy robe, which was loose enough to fit over the "Maiden." Mrs. Graff said, "Oh, Dr. Dooley, I'm so happy to meet you. . . . I admire your work so much. . . . You are a fine young man!" He smiled sadly and said, "Dear lady, I'm just a tired old man." And, at that moment, he was indeed.

The next day he rested with a heating pad and had a massage, but nothing really helped. He was taking his drugs very sparingly, because he had appointments with the Cambodian Minister of Health on Monday, and wanted to have a clear mind. He promised to come here for lunch after that meeting with the minister.

At eleven o'clock on Monday morning the bell rang. When I opened the door, I almost fainted. Ted Werner was half-supporting Tom, and Tom was paper-white! We got him into bed and he rested a bit, then he told us of the frustrating day. There had been some minor misunderstanding between Medico and the Cambodian government, but it made his last day in Phnom Penh one of the worst. He took a shower, while the rest of us ate lunch.

Then he ate two bowls of fruit compote and rested. He told us he was determined to depart that afternoon (December 19) as scheduled for Bangkok where he had more negotiating to do with the government of Thailand. Then he wanted to be in Laos for Christmas.

John ordered a big car to take Tom to the airport because our little British Ford had been too uncomfortable for him since he began wearing the brace. Ted and I agreed to go ahead to the airport with the luggage and passports so that everything would be ready when Tom arrived. Meanwhile, he would rest, with Dr. Clint Chambers watching over him, until the last moment before departure.

John had to go to the office, so he said goodbye at our house. Tom had tears in his eyes when John shook hands with him. They had been friends and rivals since those glorious days back in La Porte, Indiana, when we were all sixteen years old.

Tom said, "John, for someone who never liked me, you've been so patient." John said, "Why, Tom, I've always like you. . . . I just was mad when you took all the girls eighteen years ago!" Tom smiled and said, "Yeah, but look who's sleeping alone now."

We left him with Dr. Chambers, and Ted and I went on to the airport. Ted had many papers to fill out to clear the plane, so I took Tom's luggage through customs and cleared his passport. There I ran into trouble. Tom had a visa for three days. He had arrived on the fifteenth and this was the nineteenth. The Cambodian inspector was not going to let him go.

I cried, and they called for the director. He was the only one who could straighten out the matter, and he was out to lunch. I began to get frantic. It assumed the proportions of a tragedy with slapstick overtones—uniformed men trying to calm me down, trying to find the director, looking alternately stern and helpless.

Just then, Tom walked in through the gate. The customs men took one look at him, wearing his ghastly brace and obviously in agony. The inspector merely picked up his stamp and marked the visa. Not another word was said.

We walked out onto the apron of the field, where Ted had the plane ready. As we walked along Tom said, "I hope I haven't hurt anyone's feelings. . . . I've felt so mean lately . . . and I have so much to do. . . . I thought I'd have more time. I love these boys, my teams. . . . I hope they will understand. I love you and John. . . . I hope you both will forgive me for all the trouble I've caused you."

Just as he was ready to board the plane, he discovered that he didn't have his demerol. This caused another frantic episode. The luggage was unloaded and the suitcases searched. We couldn't find the painkiller anywhere, and we knew he would need it. There was nothing to do but load up and take off. Tom stood for a moment and said, "I wonder if I can get by without it." Then he straightened up a little, grinned, and climbed on board. The door was slammed closed. Then, just after Ted started up the engines, Tom peered through the window grinning and waving his little tin box of demerol! We stood and watched the plane until it was out of sight.

*December 20-23.* Ted Werner remembers these pre-Christmas days in Bangkok only vaguely and in a jumble of impressions that were part of a nightmare:

When we arrived on the evening of the nineteenth, Tom was in bad shape. The ride in from the airport was a torture, and he screamed at the driver for going too fast over the bumpy road. He was exhausted by the time we reached the Erawan Hotel, but even the effort to get into and out of bed was too much, so he decided it would be easier for him if I took the mattress and sheets off and made up a bed on the floor.

The next morning he was worse, so I arranged for a doctor of the Seventh-Day Adventists Hospital to give him diathermy treatments, and that seemed to help some. There was so much that he was committed to do in Bangkok—people to be seen, negotiations with the Thai government to be completed, drugs and equipment to be requisitioned and shipped. Tom's days of hurry and drive were over, so I had to pitch in and do the best I could by following his instructions. Meanwhile, I had to have the plane overhauled and, just in case he insisted upon making the flight to Muong Sing and Ban Houei Sai, I had the extra seats removed and an air mattress installed.

On December 23, it was obvious that he couldn't make the trip to Laos, so he ordered me to fly up and bring Doctors Ronald Wintrob and Estelle Hughes to Bangkok.

On the evening of December 23, Father John Boucher answered the telephone in the Redemptorist Fathers' rectory of the Holy Redeemer Church on Ruem Rudi Lane in Bangkok.

"Father, this is Tom Dooley. Can you come over and give me Communion? I'm at the Erawan Hotel. Room 101. Don't ask any questions at the desk because they won't tell you a thing. Nobody knows I'm here. Just walk in."

As he quickly packed his sick-call set, Father Boucher thought how weak and labored Tom Dooley's voice had sounded. He had heard reports that Dr. Dooley was suffering from a recurrence of his cancer and that he was making a last round of his stations. But he didn't know how bad things were!

"What I found in Room 101 shocked me. Tom was lying on the floor of his room on a hard mattress, alone, suffering. His face was pale and drawn. There was a rosary in his hand. Next to him on the bed lay the heavy back-brace which he called his 'Iron Maiden.' The telephone was on the floor beside him."

Dooley greeted the priest with a weak gesture and tried to smile. He made an attempt to move himself into a more comfortable position and grimaced. "Father, pardon me, but I cannot use the bed. My back hurts too much. They're flying me out of here as soon as possible. I'm not sure when, but I wanted to make sure I would receive Communion for Christmas."

Father Boucher asked him why he wasn't in a hospital.

"They can't do anything more for me. . . . I just want to be alone, Father. Only a few people know I'm here."

Father Boucher realized that Tom Dooley was a very sick man.

"Tom, I don't want to alarm you, but I think it might be wise for me to give you Extreme Unction. You're not really dying yet but I don't have to tell you about your condition. Maybe Extreme Unction might help you."

Then Father Boucher saw that the suggestion had shocked Tom Dooley. "For a moment Tom looked at me without saying a word. Of course, he knew that the sacrament was by no means a toll of death and that very often it had the effect of restoring physical as well as spiritual well-being. All the same, I am sure that he was shaken for one brief moment. I could see it in his eyes, and he whispered, 'Please, Father, give it to me.'"

Throughout the ceremony, Father Boucher recalls,

231

Tom seemed entirely relaxed and resigned. "Whatever terror or shock he may have experienced in the preceding few moments disappeared entirely. Tom was alone and at peace with his God."

*Christmas Eve.* Father Boucher returned early in the morning and again gave Tom Dooley Communion. He seemed much worse. Yet he perked up and made a surprising request.

"Father, I must ask a great favor of you. Could you arrange for them to save a place for me tonight at midnight Mass? Preferably in the rear of the choir loft, where I can slip in unobserved? I think I can make it, and this may be my last."

Father Boucher promised, and that day the Redemptorists placed a special chair in a corner of the choir loft, and arranged for someone to be on watch for his arrival. "Of course, he never came, and I never thought he would," Father Boucher says.

Christmas Eve was one of Tom's worst days. Dr. Ronald Wintrob was to be one of the very few who saw Dooley during his last agonizing hours in Southeast Asia. He arrived at the Erawan Hotel with Ted Werner and Estelle Hughes.

"There was no doubt then that he was dying—he would be dead within three months, I thought. Tom looked like the typical terminal cancer case—terribly thin and with an unhumanly white, sunken face. He was in constant pain, shifting about on the mattress, trying to find a more comfortable position, but without success. It shocked me to see such a complete collapse in a man in only four weeks."

Ted Werner completed arrangements for Tom to leave Bangkok via Pan American the next day (Christmas) for New York. The arrangements were complicated because Ted insisted upon two seats located in the front of the plane with the dividing arm-rests removed. He wanted special wiring for a heating pad since no plug-in outlets were available.

Dr. Estelle Hughes spent most of the day with Dooley. She sat quietly in the room, which was filled with flowers, quietly opening and sorting Tom's Christmas cards and making a list of the senders for the records in New York. His only visitors besides Dr. Estelle, were Werner, Wintrob and two people from the embassy. Late in the afternoon there was a flurry in the lobby and corridor of the hotel and Tom had an unexpected caller—Pote Sarasin.

"Mr. Sarasin seemed to be the only one who aroused Dr. Dooley's spirits that whole day," says Doctor Estelle. "He stayed for over an hour, and when he tried to leave, Dr. Dooley, although obviously in great pain, begged him to stay a little longer. They talked a great deal about the political problems and the future of Laos."

But when Pote Sarasin left, Tom lapsed back into his torments. "He made all of us leave the room, as he

233

always did when the pain became unbearable, because he never wanted any of us to see him suffer."

"That night," says Dr. Hughes, "Tom Dooley was unaware that it was Christmas Eve.

On Christmas morning, Father Boucher brought Tom Communion for the last time.
The room seemed darker and more oppressive than before, he recalls:

> This time I found Tom deeply depressed and in extreme pain. "Pax huic domui," I prayed and arranged the Blessed Sacrament on the small table. Then, disregarding the rubrics, I turned to him and said, "Merry Christmas, Tom." He tried to smile, but I could see there was something bothering him, so I waited for him to speak.
>
> "You wished me a Merry Christmas, Father. I can't help thinking that this is my last. And it's not a very merry one, is it? Not a very merry one at all, and yet somehow I feel resigned and peaceful. If this is the way God wants it to be, this is the way I want it, too."
>
> He paused a moment. "Sorry I couldn't make midnight Mass, Father. Last night was a pretty bad one."
>
> I tried to say a few words of assurance, then I gave him Communion. But his words stuck in my mind. Here was a young man in the prime of life, at the peak of his career, saying a thing like that. A couple of thousand years ago a Man of the same age spoke almost the same words in the Garden of Gethsemani: "Father, if it be Thy Will let this Chalice pass from me. Nevertheless not my will but Thine be done."

As I gave him Communion, Tom cried softly. The rosary was still in his hand. He seemed to be never without that rosary. After a few moments of silent prayer he held out his hand to me.

"I'm leaving tonight for New York. So long, Father, and thanks for everything. Remember me in your prayers, please."

I stayed on a few minutes to pray with him, then we started chatting, although it was obvious that conversation was a real effort for him, and I had no intention of remaining more than a moment. This is when a very strange thing happened.

For some reason I mentioned the word "Medico" and all of a sudden Tom sat up, his eyes brightened and for the next four or five minutes he became a changed man. This was the old Tom Dooley, with all his youth and enthusiasm and machine-gun chatter. This was Tom Dooley the crusader, face alive, pain forgotten, eloquent, determined, convincing.

I sat there amazed. He told me all about Medico, as though I had never heard of it before. He talked about its beginnings, progress, present state, and his dreams for its future. He even told me about the stations he had yet to visit on this tour. "I've got to keep them going, Father. It's important that I go to them. Perhaps, somehow, God will let me do it."

Then suddenly he stopped talking, sank back on the pillow and a grimace of pain came over his face, and tears moistened his eyes. After a moment of silence I knew it was time to leave. I gave him my blessing and walked out of the room. But those few minutes left an unforgettable impression on me. I thought to myself: how dedicated can a person become? This man was

not only dedicated, he lived and breathed his dedication. He was dedication personified. This is what gave
him his true greatness, and Dr. Tom Dooley was truly
a great man.

On Christmas night Estelle Hughes sat alone with
Tom Dooley as they waited for Ted Werner to return
from the airport where he was making final arrangements for Tom's departure. Dooley was wearing only
light khaki trousers and shirt; it was now too painful
for him to change clothes. He dismissed Estelle's warn-
ing that it would be cold when he arrived in New
York: "They'll have plenty of blankets." He had not
eaten anything for days, but now he told Estelle that
he would like an ice cream cone, which she ordered
for him. He was nibbling on the cone when Ted
Werner returned.

"Everything is ready," Ted reported. "But Pan
American is distressed because you are making the
long trip alone. They even offered me free passage if
I could go with you. I told them I could afford to pay
my own way, but you would not allow me to go."

Dooley answered irritably: "Ted, we've been over
all this a dozen times! I intend to go alone, so don't
mention it again. And I hope you warned Pan Am
that I don't want any fuss or publicity. If they put my
name on that damn VIP list this time it will be terrible. Just cable Malcolm and tell him to be standing

by in New York. No one is to know anything about my arrival."

They walked out of the hotel, with Ted carrying the one small handbag Dooley would take with him. Tom refused to let anyone hold his good left arm, and he insisted on getting into the car, slowly and painfully, all by himself.

On the way to the airport, he gave Ted Werner specific instructions: "Now when we get to the plane, let me get out and make it on my own. You can come aboard with me, but don't take my arm. Just keep close enough so that I can lean on you, if necessary. But if I do, just bolster me up, don't try to grab me."

And that's the way it was. Tom Dooley went up the steps without mishap and Ted Werner was by his side. The departure had been delayed for his benefit, so the farewells had to be brief. Ted saw him to the double seat that had been arranged for him at the front of the first-class section. Tom held out his hand. "Goodbye, Ted, and thanks for everything, old boy. God bless you."

Ted hurried down the ramp, and saw the door close. The big 707 taxied out to the runway and took off. Thus Tom Dooley departed from Southeast Asia for the last time.

How many air miles Tom Dooley traveled in 1955-60, by commercial planes alone, is almost anyone's guess.

But the people at Pan Am think he must have held some sort of record. At any rate, he had a reputation on the airlines.

He was a sleepless and gregarious traveler who made many new friends aboard planes. He talked to his seat-mate, and when his seat-mate wearied and went to sleep, Tom would move to the airliner's lounge, if there was one, and there he would talk to the stay-ups. When the stay-ups went back to their seats to sleep, he remained and talked to any crew member available, and always to the tireless stewardess. Dooley respected and adored airline stewardesses, and particularly those on the international runs, as a breed apart.

But on his last flight things were different. The relatively few passengers on Pan American's Bangkok to New York flight on December 25, 1960, knew only that the passenger who occupied both forward seats on the left side of de luxe section was a sick man. They saw that he neither could sit nor lie down for very long. He was up and down, and for brief periods he even stretched out on the floor. And he required almost constant attention from the crew.

Purser Dan Russo remembers that his condition was particularly bad on the Istanbul-Frankfort leg of the flight. "I had seen Doctor Dooley on one of our flights out of Bangkok about two years earlier, and he was then a robust man, full of vitality and animation. Meanwhile, I had read about his illness. But I was shocked when I saw him on December 26, so thin, weak, drawn and obviously dying."

Russo had instructions to keep a watch over Dr. Dooley, make him as comfortable as possible, and to see that he took medication every two hours. "I offered him food and hot drinks, but he just waved them aside with a weak, pained smile. The thing that impressed me most was his obvious desire to be as little trouble to us as possible."

When Russo reported Dooley's condition to Captain Cassmier Szmagaj (pronounced Shmaggy) during the Vienna-Frankfort leg, the captain decided that it might be advisable for Tom to spend the night in Frankfort, get medical attention and some rest, and continue on to London and New York the next day. He contacted Pan-Am-Frankfort on the company frequency and requested that arrangements be made.

"He was the most cheerful dying man I have ever seen," says Captain Szmagaj. "All of us were impressed by the cheerfulness and considerateness of this man who was obviously suffering so much. We even kidded a bit. Once, when I asked how he felt, he answered that he felt all right, and I said, 'Well, maybe you ought to be up there flying the plane!' Doctor Dooley said: 'I wish I could—you know, I've always wanted to learn to fly.'"

After this overnight stop in Frankfort, Tom Dooley resumed his agonizing journey home. When his plane reached London, Stewardess Erika Missler reported aboard for duty. She is a tall, graceful young woman, with loosely curled dark hair and dark eyes, and she has a slight German accent which Tom Dooley, even in his agony, found captivating. "She was such a fascinating girl," he said later, "and she was kind and understanding. I wish there had been time to learn more about her."

Erika Missler recalls:

I came on duty in London and was with him between London and New York. Fortunately we had few passengers aboard that flight and I was able to spend practically all my time with him. Normally we are so busy we can't give too much attention to any one passenger.

He was in tremendous pain. I've never seen anybody as sick as he was that night. His great problem was finding some position in which he could be comfortable. We tried everything.

The airplane had been specially wired so his heating pad could be used. Ordinarily there are no outlets near the seats so they had to extend lines from the galley to his location. He had two seats in the first row of the deluxe section. With the arm-rest removed there is enough room for a person to stretch out. Dr. Dooley's spine pained him so severely that any position was torture. He tried to lie down, then he tried to sit up; finally he lay on the floor. During the night I put him on the floor of the passenger lounge.

I felt so sorry for the man because he was so completely helpless. I remember asking him: "Isn't there anything you can take to relieve the pain?" He said that he had been taking drugs consistently, but then he took some more pills. He said, "These pills no longer even touch the pain." I wondered: Would the pain be even worse if you took no drugs at all? That was inconceivable because he was already in unbearable agony. That was obvious. I really admired the man and his self-control.

He couldn't sleep, and I could see he wanted to talk but couldn't. Everything was such an effort for him. We didn't converse much. It was mostly "Do you want your legs up? Shall we try putting your legs down? Don't you want to eat something?" He hadn't eaten anything. I finally talked him into having a few slices of roast beef, and later he sipped a little hot chocolate.

I filled out his customs form, took his passport, and he showed me some pictures that had been taken months before. He told me he had lost something like 36 pounds in the two preceding weeks. He was so skinny—all bones.

I felt so helpless, because I am not a nurse. I asked him, "Isn't there *anything* I can do?" He said, "Well, I don't suppose stewardesses are trained to give massages, are they?" "Well, no," I said, "we aren't trained nurses, and I'm not much good at it, but I'll try if you think it will help." But even gentle massages didn't help, because his back was so sensitive to the touch. He would get cramps in the muscles right down his side.

When the seat belt sign flashed on, I had to check the plane and ask all passengers to sit up and strap themselves in. It seemed so ridiculous in Dr. Dooley's case, but he sat up and fastened the belt, and I sat beside him.

We were making an instrument approach to Idlewild and it took us *ages* to come in. We circled and circled, and I could see the lights of Idlewild Terminal. Dr. Dooley just couldn't sit upright with his seat belt fastened. It was killing him. Yet, during this time, he asked me what my name was, and where I came from. About four weeks later I got a letter from someone at Medico [Teresa Gallagher] saying that one of the first things Dr. Dooley mentioned when he landed was to suggest a letter thanking me for my help on that flight. Can you imagine a person in his condition thinking of that!

When we landed, at last, the plane taxied to an area where they had a special ramp waiting for him, and I saw the cars and an ambulance. He insisted upon getting off alone, although he was almost bent over double with pain. He thanked me, and said good-bye, and added, "I must get off this plane alone and on my own two feet." As he left, I thought, "There goes a brave man."

*December 27.* While the plane circled over Idlewild, Malcolm Dooley, his wife, Gay, Teresa Gallagher and Russ Stewart of Medico arrived and were met by the Pan American representatives. It was snowing heavily, and their taxi had broken down halfway out of New York.

"Fortunately," says Teresa, "we had left early, and a vacant cab came up right behind us. But the roads were lined with stalled cars. When we arrived we heard that the pilot had called the Idlewild tower and ordered an ambulance for Tom. Mrs. Dooley had telephoned me from St. Louis the day before and asked if there would be a wheelchair ready for him. That sounded ghastly—I couldn't imagine Tom Dooley in a wheelchair. But now, when they spoke of an ambulance, the wheelchair sounded like a pretty good idea. However, I was still hoping and praying that he would arrive standing up.

They got into a rented limousine and drove around the field, escorted by a patrol car with a flashing red beacon, and followed by the ambulance. The patrol car led them to an area near the end of the assigned runway where they were to wait.

"That awful period of waiting for the plane to land became almost unbearable," Teresa says, "because we knew he was up there in the overcast, and yet we had to wonder how he was and what condition he was in. I remember how bitterly I resented the nonchalance of the ambulance driver and his assistant who were just sitting there talking and smoking as if nothing were wrong."

At last the plane landed and taxied up to the waiting cars. Arrangements had been made for Tom Dooley to disembark by special ramp from the front of the plane.

"Thank God! He stepped out onto the platform unassisted," says Teresa. "He was bent over, with his hands holding his back, and he was obviously in excruciating pain. But he paused and said goodbye to the hostess. We were waiting at the foot of the ramp as he came down the steps slowly and painfully. He took one look at the ambulance standing there with doors open and stretcher ready, and said, "I won't need that. I'll ride in your car."

They gave him the wide, well-cushioned rear seat. Malcolm and Gay sat on the jump-seats and tried to make him comfortable, and Teresa rode forward with the chauffeur. The limousine cruised out of the serpentine roads leading from Idlewild, and then sped toward New York over the snow-covered highway. Teresa Gallagher remembers glancing at the speedometer and seeing the indicator move from 75 to 80 miles per hour.

Tom shifted painfully in the back seat. He didn't groan or complain, but tried to make conversation, mostly in gasped questions and brief replies. He asked Gay about the children and was told they were fine.

"And how are you, Tess?"

"Tom, I've just been fine."

"God bless you, Tess. What would I do without you? Tess, make a note. Remind me to write to that stewardess, Miss Erika Missler—E-r-i-k-a M-i-s-s-l-e-r. She was wonderful to me."

Malcolm said that there was a lot of criticism and resentment because he had been allowed to make the long trip alone.

"That's the way I wanted it, Mal. And thanks for doing everything as I asked. I know that ambulance wasn't your idea."

Malcolm said the pilot had ordered it, and Tom

244

almost chuckled. "Yes, they really thought they were going to have to take me off feet first."

The chauffeur sped west on eastbound 68th Street and stopped directly in front of Memorial Hospital. Tom got out of the limousine and walked up the steps, slowly but unassisted, with his hands in the back pockets of his wrinkled khaki trousers. He was escorted directly to his room on the ninth floor and practically collapsed on the divan.

He ordered some things he wanted—a bedboard, plenty of pillows, hot water bottles. They also brought in a frame which was rigged over the bed so that he could pull himself upright or lower himself into a reclining position.

"That pulley arrangement became the measure of Tom's decline," says Teresa Gallagher. "At first he could use it to shift around and try to make himself comfortable. But gradually the exertion became too much and it was painful even to see him try."

The year ended on a somber note. On December 31 word reached Medico in New York that, because of the chaotic conditions in northern Laos, the American team, headed by Dr. Ronald Wintrob had been evacuated from Muong Sing and sent to Ban Houei Sai. When the cablegram was shown to Tom Dooley he was heartbroken.

# PART SIX

# 1961:

# JANUARY

The story of the darkening days in January 1961 is told best by Tom Dooley's devoted and tireless Teresa Gallagher, who never failed to come to Room 910 before she went to work each morning, during most of her lunch hours, and every evening for as long as the doctors and nurses would let her stay. This is Teresa's story:

We tried to schedule our visits so that there would never be too many people there at the same time. My principal chore was to take care of the mail that came to the hospital, and there was so much of it that I laid in a supply of shopping bags. He dictated letters up until New Year's Eve, but after that it became too much for him.

He talked constantly about wanting to work on a new book which he intended to call *The Night of the Same Day*. But then he said: "Oh, what's the use, Tess, I'll be dead in a month's time."

"You're not going to die in a month, Tom," I argued. I really thought he might last six months. "If you want to start work on your book, I'll be glad to help you."

249

We did talk a bit about it and I saw the folder of material he had gathered. I was completely bewildered, first because I didn't know anything about writing a book, and secondly because the material was a conglomeration of anecdotes, random thoughts, philosophizing, bits of poetry, and special letters he had received from various people. We never did get started on it.

Tom got progressively worse almost from the day he entered the hospital. After they started radiation therapy he became terribly nauseated, and as his pains became more and more severe his sedation had to be increased and he seemed to grow more detached. Yet he would call me up at the office almost every day to tell me about something he wanted.

Once he called me and asked me to bring him a hot dog—and it had to be from Nedick's! I knew how he liked hot dogs and he could always tell a Nedick's frankfurter from any other—you couldn't fool him. That evening I looked all over and couldn't find a Nedick's stand open in mid-town. I finally found one— about forty-five or more blocks from the hospital. The real problem was how to keep the hot dog hot until I reached the hospital. Perhaps it sounds silly, but I would have flown to Washington or Boston and back if necessary to get Tom the Nedick's hot dog he wanted that night.

I remember another day when he called and said: "Tess, I can't find my brace. Will you see where it is?"

I thought: What has happened? He can't find his brace. For a moment I thought he meant the brace he had brought from Hong Kong, the "Iron Maiden," which was an awful thing. Then I recalled that they were making a new brace at Memorial, and I decided that was what he had called me about. I finally found the secretary of the man who was making it and she said it would probably be sent to the hospital that day. I had thought that perhaps Tom was under the influence of drugs when he called, but he was absolutely right. The brace had been promised for that day and he knew it. When I got to Memorial that evening the brace had been delivered.

Tom was quite proud of his new brace and he tried sitting up in the red leather chair. But getting up and down was difficult, and he could not remain in the chair for long.

"Tom," I said, "instead of trying to get out of bed to sit in that chair, have you ever thought of getting a cushioned bed rest? You could sit up in bed and be more comfortable." He seemed interested in the suggestion, so our Dooley Aid Club decided to give him a bed rest for his birthday.

My friend Kathleen and I went to Bloomingdale's and got the huge cushion shaped like an armchair. When I brought it up to the room the nurse looked at it and shook his head.

"Not so good?" I asked. "You mean he can't even use this?"

"I don't think it's possible," he said. "But put it in the room. We'll let him try it anyway." (He never was able to use it.)

One side of Tom's face had now become paralyzed. His sight was affected, and he had to wear a black patch over his right eye. On January 11 the doctors informed Malcolm that the cancer was spreading rapidly into almost every organ, including the brain. Tom's time

251

was very short. The question was how much of the truth he should be told. When I heard that the consensus was to tell Tom everything I was horrified.

I caught one of the doctors in the corridor. "Please, I beg you, don't do it—even though you are a doctor and you do know the end is near. Even if he is a doctor, I'm sure he would still like to think there is a little hope or a little time left."

The doctor was very patient and understanding. "My dear girl, we know how you feel. But you know Doctor Dooley too well to ask us to do anything different. He wants to be told the truth. He made us promise. This is *his* wish."

Malcolm said: "The doctor is right, Teresa. Besides, we have reason to believe that for a long time Tom has known everything."

Then I knew they were right. Tom knew more of the truth than even they could tell him.

On January 16, the day before his birthday, a big white cake with lots of blue carnations on it arrived from someone in St. Louis. It was very attractive. I showed it to Tom. He stuck his finger in the icing and said, "I'll have a piece of that in about two hours." The nurse made a note of it.

Meanwhile an old gentleman in San Francisco named Arthur Haugh had written and asked me to order a special cake for Tom. It had to be all chocolate and decorated with an Irish harp and shamrocks. I thought of Ann Walsh and the chef at the Waldorf, not knowing that the Waldorf chef already had been commissioned to make a cake for Tom—a beautiful thing with a huge gold candle. It looked like a glorified merry-go-round. Nevertheless, we had the chocolate cake made to

Mr. Haugh's specifications and both cakes were delivered to Memorial. When I got there we put the gold candle on one cake and lighted it, but Tom wasn't able to try it. He was just too sick.

Tom's wonderful mother [who had been in New York for several weeks] was exhausted by this time, and on January 16 Malcolm and the doctors persuaded her to return to St. Louis for a few days, since she was not in good health herself. Yet Mrs. Dooley is a very sensitive woman, and she expressed the fear that Tom might not live through his birthday. Malcolm assured her that if anything happened he would telephone and she could be back in New York within a few hours. As things turned out, it seemed providential that she was safely home when the terrible blizzard turned everything into chaos during the next few days.

His birthday was Tuesday, January 17. I went to the hospital at noontime. I went into the room but Tom didn't recognize me.

"Tom, is there anything I can do for you?" I asked.

He kept pointing to various things, and talking incoherently. I felt sure he had something on his mind, something he wanted me to do. But the words and gestures were meaningless and it was plain that he didn't know who I was. It was heartbreaking.

[Bob Copenhaver had had a somewhat similar experience a few days earlier. When Bob heard the doctors' verdict on January 11, he flew from Omaha to New York. "When I saw Tom it took him fully five minutes to recognize me. Then he was under the impression that we were on the lecture tour again. We were all set to to go to Pittsfield that night. He wanted me to go on ahead to the airport and save him a seat in the lounge of the plane. When I started to leave the room he told me that he would follow as soon as he had a chance to bathe and shave. That was the last time I saw him alive."]

On his birthday [Teresa continues] as we were leaving the hospital I met Monsignor Wilders, the chaplain of New York Hospital, in the lobby. I introduced Kathleen, and he said, "Why don't you girls wait. Cardinal Spellman is coming up to see Dr. Dooley."

We both looked at our watches. We had to be back at the office, but Malcolm called my boss from the lobby and I got the afternoon off. After we greeted the Cardinal, we went up to Room 910. Tom recognized Cardinal Spellman immediately. He rose up in bed and made the Lao *sathoo* sign of greeting, with his hands before his face and head bowed. His Eminence remained alone with Tom for some time, and when he came out he had tears in his eyes. He said: "I tried to assure him that in his 34 years he had done what very few have done in the allotted Scriptural lifetime."

I had a long standing engagement to give a talk about Medico to the American Legion Post in our company on Thursday evening, January 19. Public speaking is an ordeal for me, but I was doing this for Tom. Because of this meeting I felt that I should go home early on the night of the 18th and get some sleep. I knew that Malcolm was going to the hospital around six o'clock before attending a Medico meeting, and I felt that Tom probably wouldn't miss me.

But I had three letters that he had dictated on the previous Sunday. He had signed the first one fine, but the second signature looked bad and he'd gotten completely confused on the third. I couldn't send the two letters that way so I had decided to do them over and sign them myself. As I was retyping them I said to myself, "I bet these are the last letters I'm ever going to do for him." The more I thought about it, the worse I felt. When I finished the second letter I signed and mailed it and decided I couldn't possibly go home without going to the hospital and seeing if he needed anything.

When I got to the hospital I saw Tony, the nurse, and asked him how Tom was. He said, "Not so good."

"His condition is fair on the records," I said. "Has anybody been in?"

"No, he's been resting quietly."

We went into the room. Tony had Tom raised up quite high in the bed and I asked, "Tony, is he comfortable that way?"

"I'll change him any way you want."

"Oh, you're the nurse. Don't let me interfere. I just wonder if he's comfortable."

"Well, I'll lower it a bit." So Tony lowered the bed. I guess it was about 7:30 at the time.

I then asked Tony, "How's his blood pressure? How's his pulse?"

Tony said, "His blood pressure is 130 and his pulse is strong and regular."

I kept looking at Tom and felt that I had to say a prayer for him. He looked so sick. So I started to say my rosary aloud while Tony stood in the doorway. While I was saying the rosary, Tom's hand went up as if he were signifying his approval of what I was doing. Perhaps it was just a meaningless motion, but this is how I interpreted it. I continued praying, and I kept wishing there was a priest there to say the prayers for

255

the dying. Not that I really thought Tom was dying
because the chart said that his condition was fair. I
circled the bed and looked at him and felt his forehead.
It seemed so cold to me. "Tony," I asked, "when was
the doctor here last?"

"You met him on the way up," he said.

"Was that the doctor?"

"Yes."

"What did he say?"

Tony told me the doctor had just said there was no
indication of any change. I started putting Tom's mail
in the shopping bags, hoping that he wasn't hearing
all the noise. I put all the papers and bags out in the
corridor. When I came back I noticed a card lying on
the table.

"Where did this come from?" I asked Tony.

"Father Muller, the chaplain, left it."

"Did he leave any instructions?"

"No, he just left it in case you might need it."

I picked up the card and kept walking around with it
in my hand. Finally I said, "I'm going to call this priest
and ask him to come over and say a rosary with me."

"Would you want the doctor?" Tony asked.

"Tony, I hope I'm doing the right thing. I'm not a
member of the family, and I don't want to make a fuss
about this. But he looks so sick."

Tony said. "It will be perfectly all right for me to
call a doctor. We have a young doctor on call. Let me
get him."

The doctor came and took Tom's pulse and said he
was breathing all right. As he was doing this, the little
walkie-talkie in his pocket kept going off. He did what

he could do and then beckoned to me and we went out into the hall.

"How is he?" I asked. "I'd like to call a priest."

He asked me, "What list is he on?"

"I don't know what you're talking about."

"Well, what did the report say?"

"I don't know. I think they said his condition was fair."

The doctor called someone and then hung up. He was sitting on a table in the laundry room opposite Tom's room. He said: "They say he was 'poor' this afternoon but 'fair' this evening."

"What does that mean?"

"Well, usually you don't send for a priest unless the patient is on the critical list, and he's not on the critical list. But if you want to send for the priest that's all right. You have that privilege."

"Well, I hope people won't think he's on the critical list just because I send for a priest." I was afraid something might get into the newspapers. I didn't want to upset Medico's plans. I just didn't know what to do.

I went to the phone and called Father Mueller. He was at evening devotions. I called again and couldn't reach him. I went back and looked at Tom and felt his forehead. I thought: He really is sick . . . so sick it doesn't seem right to leave him.

"Do you think I ought to go home and come back?" I asked Tony. "Or if I call you at midnight will you tell me how he's doing then?"

"You can call me any time," Tony said.

I decided to phone once more. This time Father Muller answered.

"Father," I said, "I think you should come over and see Dr. Dooley."

"All right," Father Muller said. "I'll be right over."

As I was sitting there making the phone call to the priest, the floor nurse came by and said, "While you're there, Miss Gallagher, you'd better call his brother."

"What do you mean?"

"I mean exactly that."

"Is it that bad?"

"Tell him to come here as soon as possible."

I tried to reach Malcolm, but he had left the meeting and had not yet reached his home. I went back toward the room, and saw the priest coming down the hall. We went in, and I knelt beside the bed while he read the prayers and anointed Tom. Since hearing is the last thing that goes, at the end of the sacrament of Extreme Unction the priest bends over and whispers into the ear: "Son, go now and meet thy God." Those words will remain in my mind for the rest of my life.

Fortunately I had been with my father when he died, so this wasn't a new experience for me. Otherwise, I doubt that I could have taken it.

Tony kept patting Tom gently on the shoulder and saying, "Are you all right, Doc? Do you need anything, Doc?" Tom wasn't able to answer.

Father Muller called me out into the hall. "Don't get alarmed," he told me. "I'm a chaplain of James Ewing Hospital [part of Memorial Center] and I see these cases all the time. After the sacrament of Extreme Unction is administered, the patient usually experiences great peace and tranquillity and feels very calm. Don't mistake it for anything else. And don't talk in the room, because he can hear anything you're saying. If you have anything to say to the nurse, say it out in the hall."

"Thank you, Father. I'll walk with you to the elevator." We got halfway down the hall and he said, "You don't have to come the rest of the way, Miss Gallagher. I have to report this to the desk, and it's not necessary for you to come along."

"Whatever you say, Father. Thank you for coming."

He went on down the hall and I went back to Tom. I went directly to the head of the bed and looked at him. There was obvious tranquillity, obvious peace. "Father Muller certainly was right," I said to myself. "And, thank God. He seems so much more peaceful and at rest."

I was standing right there watching him breathe so much more easily. He seemed to be more comfortable. Tony was standing right next to me. Suddenly I realized that Tom *wasn't* breathing!

"Tony," I said, "Tony, did Tom just die?" Tony reached for Tom's pulse and then nodded. There had been no gasping, no thrashing, nothing. There was just a quiet, peaceful slipping away.

My immediate reaction was "God is good." I was grateful that he had gone so easily, that he had gone with the rites of his own church, and that he wasn't all alone. I might have been in the hall. I couldn't understand why I had been there. I never intended to be there. He had come so far and in so much pain to be in New York with the people who loved him and wanted to be with him. And to think that he might have died alone!

Tom Dooley died at 9:45 P.M. on Wednesday, January 18, 1961. The autopsy, performed as he had requested, revealed at last the extent of his disease and the depth of his suffering. The malignant melanoma had spread to his lungs, brain, liver, spleen, heart—no organ had been spared. The marrow in his bones was supplanted almost completely by tumor.

That night the lowering clouds promised snow. A low pressure area that had built up in southern Virginia was moving north through West Virginia, Maryland and Pennsylvania. By 11:25 on Thursday morning the thermometer dropped to 12 degrees and the first flakes fell on New York City. By Thursday night New York—and most of the East—lay under a blanket of snow with drifts reaching 21 inches at some points.

The massive storm of January 19-20 enormously complicated plans for Tom Dooley's funeral in St. Louis. Bob Copenhaver, summoned to active duty for the last time, tells the story:

About 12:30 A.M. on Thursday (January 19) the telephone rang at my bedside. I knew instinctively what the call was, but I knew I was too groggy to respond intelligently so I just let the phone ring and ring.

My wife asked: "Why don't you answer it?"

"I know what it is," I said. "Tom's dead. That's Malcolm calling. I want to get every word he says."

I picked up the phone and in a brusque, tired manner Mal said, "Tom is dead. It was peaceful. About two or three hours ago. Teresa was with him at the time."

"I knew it," I said.

"Could you go to St. Louis tomorrow? We hope for a

260

Monday funeral. Crawford King is helping there. I've made reservations for you at the Chase Hotel."

"I'll be there."

"We want everything as Tom would have it—the full treatment. The people will want to see him, so we hope we can get the Cathedral—the body to lie in state on Sunday."

"What about the press?" I asked.

"Just as Tom would have it—invite everyone."

"I'll see you at the Chase tomorrow evening."

The next evening (January 19) I flew to St. Louis, but that was the day of the blizzard. When I arrived at the hotel a wire from Malcolm awaited me. I called him at International Hotel at Idlewild Airport. They were snowbound. While we were talking, a Mexican airliner crashed within sight of their hotel window.

Malcolm told me the body was arriving during the night, gave me the number of the TWA flight, and asked me to meet the plane and take the body to the funeral home. He was skeptical about the cargo flight ever making it in the storm.

I went to the airport in the 15 degree, windy, snowy weather, and waited from 11:00 P.M until 3:00 A.M. They told me the flight had been canceled. I would have to check the next day on a rescheduled arrival time.

During Friday, January 20, I went out to the cemetery with Crawford King, looking at the grave site, studying the plot, the position of Tom's father and Earle, and helping Crawford decide which individual plot he would recommend to Mrs. Dooley. In the afternoon we saw her. I'll never forget her first words, or, rather, the way she said them.

"Bob, I'm glad to see you're here helping with every-thing—as usual—all of the details Tom never wanted to worry about." She said it as though I had been there for a month and was going to be around for a year. She was outwardly calm, but good friends were staying with her every minute of the time. She refused to get maudlin, knowing Tom would be furious with her if she did.

Crawford and I then went out and selected the casket. By this time the cargo flight was re-scheduled for that evening. Malcolm and the others were still stuck at Idlewild. That evening I met the man from the funeral home and drove out to the airport in his tired old Packard behind the hearse. The plane finally ar-rived and it must have been about 8:00 P.M. when we left the airport. It had started to snow again. The heater in the hearse didn't work nor did the defroster. Cold drafts drifted into the old Packard and we froze all the way to the funeral home.

They unloaded the pine box, and placed it in the mortuary. I had orders from Malcolm to check all mis-cellaneous items such as Tom's suit, haircut, and per-sonal belongings. A little, gnarled old man in the base-ment of the mortuary shoved a crow-bar under the lid and flipped open the box. It was a shock I'll never forget. I left, feeling ill.

It was about 10:30 P.M. when I reached the hotel and settled down to the phone calls. Most of them were inquiries from the newspapers, but I also was answering Mal's calls, some from old family friends.

For several hours I told and retold the basic story to the news media, and consoled many friends. I was tired, cold, upset. Then Malcolm, Gay, Teresa and the rest of the New York party arrived and things became more normal.

Saturday was a hectic day. I arrived at the funeral parlor shortly after mid-day and stayed until the place closed at 10:30 that night. Even at that late hour we had to fight off a crackpot who wanted Mrs. Dooley to make a statement to the effect that Tom might be alive if he had taken a certain cancer cure of herbs and exercise. The old man refused to be brushed off, and had to be removed physically from the funeral home.

On Sunday thousands visited the funeral home and passed the bier. Because the storm had tied up everything, all the flowers seemed to be late in arriving; for the first few hours there were a few baskets of flowers in the lonely room, but by late afternoon there must have been at least a hundred baskets.

At 6:00 P.M. on Sunday the doors were closed, and preparations began for the trip to the Cathedral where Tom would lie in state. The undertaker asked Mrs. Dooley to remove Tom's valuables, and she gave Tom's watch to Paul Hellmuth and his star-sapphire ring to me.

"Bob, this ring was given to Tom by his father and it was his most cherished possession. He never was without it. He would want you to have it, and he would want you to wear it—not put it in a safe-deposit box."

Even then, I guess I showed no emotion. Behind my back, I heard people calling me an "iron man"—some with admiration, and others because they thought I was cold and callous.

I accompanied the body to the Cathedral, and watched the thousands and thousands file by the bier. Many times that evening I thought, Tom, this is the best performance you've ever given. I watched the faces of the thousands who passed by, and I saw almost every emotion in the human heart—anger that he should die, pity, sorrow, tears, and the puzzled expressions of little children. I wasn't the only one who watched the spectacle and was deeply moved. One prominent newscaster fought back the tears and then just gave up and cried until his TV make-up washed away.

Two Navy men stood as honor guards beside the bier. Neither knew who Tom Dooley was; they just had been sent there on orders by the Navy Department.

"Who was this guy, anyway?" one sailor whispered to me. I couldn't explain, so I just said he was Dr. Thomas A. Dooley, formerly of the Navy Medical Corps.

"Aw, no," he said. "No doctor would ever rate this kind of a reception!"

I remained there that Sunday night until they closed the Cathedral doors. Then I went outside and all at once the pent-up emotions of the past few days tore loose. I stood on the Cathedral steps in the dark and cried until the tears frosted on my cheeks. It seemed as though I was aware, for the first time, that Tom Dooley was dead.

Early on the morning of January 23, the Dooley family, Bob Copenhaver and a few friends went to the chapel of the Cathedral to witness Khamphan Panya, Minister of Communications of Laos, representing the King, bestow upon Tom Dooley posthumously the rank of Grand Officer of the Order of the Million Elephants and the White Parasol. The decoration was placed upon a white satin pillow beside the bier.

In Tom Dooley's clasped hands rested the engraved crucifix which signified that he was an honorary (lay) member of the Order of Mary Immaculate, the Oblate Fathers, a distinction that had been conferred upon him quietly while he was in Rome in the spring of 1960. According to custom, the crucifix is taken from an Oblate Father at death and passed on to the next young priest admitted to the Order. In the rare case of a lay member, it passes to the next male in the family line. Thus this priceless heritage passed on to Tom Dooley's favorite nephew, Malcolm Dooley's son, Thomas A. Dooley IV.

The solemn pontifical mass for Tom Dooley was celebrated by the Rt. Rev. Leo C. Byrne, Bishop of St. Louis, at eleven o'clock that morning. Over two thousand people filled the Cathedral, and seated in the sanctuary were forty prelates and priests, including many representing the Oblate Fathers and the faculty of Notre Dame. Father George Gottwald, in his sermon, quoted from Robert Frost's poem, "Stopping by Woods on a Snowy Evening," the words Tom Dooley loved and lived by:

> *The woods are lovely, dark and deep.*
> *But I have promises to keep,*
> *And miles to go before I sleep.*

Tom Dooley could have enjoyed a comfortable life, said Father Gottwald; instead he chose to devote his career to ministering to the sick in far-off places. "The promises, Dr. Dooley, are fulfilled."

After the Mass, the crucifix of the Order of Mary Immaculate was removed, the white satin pillow with the Grand Officer's ribboned medal of the Order of the Million Elephants and the White Parasol was handed to an attendant. Then the pallbearers from the St. Louis University Medical School, including three Asians, carried Tom Dooley's coffin down the Cathedral steps and out into the clear, cold January sunshine.

At Calvary Cemetery, the burial service was brief. The Order of Mary Immaculate crucifix was passed to Malcolm Dooley for his son, and the Order of the Million Elephants and the White Parasol was handed to Mrs. Dooley. Then the bugler sounded taps, and they lowered Tom Dooley's coffin into the canopied grave.

# PART SEVEN

# REQUIESCAT

The news of Tom Dooley's death flashed across the time zones and around the world:

In Ludhiana, northern India, Dr. Melvin Casberg turned on the bedside radio for the morning broadcast: "There, in the quiet of our bedroom, my wife and I heard over the Voice of America that Tom had passed through the doors of death. The world had lost a great young man, but I had lost a son."

In Saigon, Madame Vu-Thi-Ngai awoke with a start. "I knew then that Tom had died," she says. "Often during my life I have had such forebodings. Later that day we heard the news on the radio. The children of An-Lac Orphanage cried and I cried with them. But I remembered what he had said: "Believe in what you are doing . . . never give up . . . work and pray."

In Quang Ngai, Al Harris and Reggie Gordon alighted from the Saigon train and found the Dr. Baa, the *médecin indochinois*, waiting for them on the platform with tears in his eyes. *"Bac Si Dooley, il est mort,"* he informed them. Al Harris says: "The next day they had a mass for Doc in the local Catholic church. There were many more Buddhists than Catholics present, and I think that was a tribute Tom would have enjoyed."

In Kenya Dr. Mungai Njoroge read the news on the front page of Nairobi's morning newspaper. "Although I had been expecting it, this came as a secondary shock. To me Tom Dooley was Medico, and Medico was Tom Dooley. Now I knew that I must work harder to make Medico a living memorial to my friend."

In Malaya Dr. Leslie Frewing was in the operating room of the Kuala Lipis hospital when a nurse whispered the message that had just been telephoned by the Minister of Health, Dato Ong. "Tom Dooley was dead! Everyone around the operating table was heartbroken," Dr. Frewing writes. "But what could we do? Carry on, of course. Tom Dooley, of all people, would not have us do otherwise."

Jeff Cheek heard the news in an officers' club on Okinawa. Someone asked him what sort of guy Dooley really was. "I wanted to tell them about Dooley," Jeff Cheek writes, "about the way he reacted to human suffering . . . about the way he always tried to help people . . . about his loneliness and his inability to communicate his real feelings . . . about the brave battle he fought . . . about the way he kept working up to the very end. . . . But now I had the problem of communication. I could only say lamely: 'You would have to know Tom Dooley to understand him. He was a good man. . . . He had many faults but his virtues outweighed them. . . . He had a heart as big—as big as this room!'"

In Vientiane, battle-scarred capital of Laos, Norman Cousins, editor of the *Saturday Review,* attended the requiem mass celebrated for Tom Dooley a few days later. His report from Laos, published in the February 4, 1961, issue of *Saturday Review,* is perhaps the most discerning comment with which to close this account of Tom Dooley's last days. We quote Norman Cousins:

> From the inside of Saint Mary's Church in Vientiane, Laos, I could see through the side door to the pocked and charred area beyond. Only a few weeks earlier the war had come this way and a dozen or more of the stilt-and-bamboo houses had burned to the ground. From outside the church, too, came the mixed sounds of the hacking coughs of old people and the staccato bragging of roosters. And, at the back of the church, standing in the open doorway, were five bicycle-rickshaw boys, caps in hand. They were peering over the heads of the congregation to the altar, where Father Matt Menger was offering requiem mass for Tom Dooley. . . .
> Father Menger spoke of Dr. Tom Dooley, his work, his beliefs, and the legacy he had left behind in Laos. He told of Dooley's last visit to St. Mary's at 5 A.M., just before he left Vientiane for the last time. And he related events that emphasized Dooley's spunky and boyish qualities. Father Menger concluded by praising the work of Medico, whose name is synonymous with

Dooley, and he prayed that Medico's work would continue and indeed expand in line with Dooley's own idea.

After the services, people stood outside in small groups for several minutes and exchanged reminiscences. Some of them wondered whether anyone would carry on Tom Dooley's work. Others speculated on the immediate fate of the two Dooley hospital stations in Laos if they should be overrun by Pathet Laos (pro-Communist) forces in the northeast.

For the time being, at least, both hospitals are safe although they are functioning with reduced personnel. The hospital station at Muong Sing, in the remote northwest corner of Laos, only a dozen miles from the Chinese border, has already been evacuated of all American personnel. The administration of the hospital has been turned over to Dooley-trained medical attendants. The second hospital, more recently established in the western corner of Laos, is only a few miles from the Thailand border; evacuation procedures have already been worked out with the Thailand government and with the hospital staff, to be put into effect on short notice.

All this is completely consistent with Dooley's own ideas. His intention from the very start was to set up a series of medical posts and turn them over to local communities. He was aware of the stern limitations involved in medical practice by field-trained personnel. In fact, much of the criticism directed against him by members of the medical fraternity was on the grounds that the quality of such medical services was bound to be atrociously low. What these critics failed to see was that many thousands of lives could be saved even on a low level of medical training. Infant mortality in Laos is more than fifty percent. By introducing simple hygienic procedures, Dooley was able to save countless numbers of children. Similarly, hundreds of Laotian women who might have died in childbirth have been saved because Dooley-trained midwives knew something about modern obstetrical techniques and recognized the importance of washing their hands. Dooley also trained his Laotian assistants to treat malarial victims, whose number in Laos is legion. They also are trained to make tests for tuberculosis and other local diseases and to administer the indicated drugs. Apart from this, they are excellent first-aid attendants and can help avoid dangerous infections.

It is perhaps significant that many of Dooley's medical critics have not come forward with alternatives; neither have they volunteered to give up their own careers to serve at any of the local jungle stations that would be turned over to local personnel. The basic fact to keep in mind is that only one fully qualified doctor was available for the entire population of Laos at the time Tom Dooley and his mission first came to Laos. There were, however, thousands of witch doctors who made their full contribution to the high death rate, especially among women in childbirth. The proper comparison, therefore, should be between medical attendants and witch doctors, and not between medical attendants and diploma-bearing skilled physicians.

Dooley was not just a doctor. He was an educator. And he knew that the success of an educator was to be measured by his ability to teach others how to pass their knowledge along. According to such a yardstick, Dooley may well have been one of the most useful teachers of his time.

Another criticism pointed at Dooley was that he him-

273

self was rather crude in his medical techniques. Dooley generally smiled when this charge was raised.

"They accuse me of practicing nineteenth century medicine," he would say. "They are absolutely correct. I do practice nineteenth century medicine, perhaps seventeenth century medicine, and it doesn't trouble me. And when I turn over a station to Laotian personnel I am sure it will be eighteen century medicine. This offers at least a little service to people who are living in the fifteenth century."

Like Albert Schweitzer, whose life and work were the inspiration that propelled the young doctor in the direction of Laos, Tom Dooley had to withstand the criticism of those who were appalled by the physical appearance of his "hospital." And, like Schweitzer, he was wise enough to know that a gleaming modern hospital in the jungle would be a waste of money; it would frighten the frayed shirts off the backs of the villagers who had never before seen anything larger than a double-sized shack.

On a non-medical basis, Dooley had the book thrown at him because of his personal manner. They said he was addicted to short cuts, got in the way of established authority, was too arbitrary, was a little too flamboyant, and was not above self-advertising. The answer, if an answer is needed, is: So what? What is important about Tom Dooley is that he tried to meet the highest need of his age or any age, which is for a sense of connection between man and man. Of course he cut corners; he had to. As Schweitzer has frequently said and as Dooley himself has repeated, anyone who has a genuine desire to serve cannot expect people to roll boulders out of his way.

Even if Dooley's mission in Asia were a total failure, which it is not, he would have valid claim to greatness because he made it possible for many thousands of people to be rescued from the cynicism and dry-eyed attitude that regards service in the cause of man as mawkish ostentation. Dooley was supremely relevant in a moral cause. He could have been the world's most temperamental man and this would not have detracted by the thinnest sliver from the magnificance of his ideas and his work. . . .